Judy -
I wanted
of my little
of my life but not revealing the
persons involved. So, it has been _sanitized_
somewhat.
I must thank you for planting the seed
to write a book. This does not compare to
what you did with your writing. You made
me aware that it was possible. So here is

BLACK BANANAS

A Memoir by

Bob White

my feeble efforts put into print. Hope
it brings some enjoyment.
Love Always,
Bob

Table of Contents

PREFACE

The beginning of this memoir, which depicts the early years of my life, is viewed through the eyes of a five-year-old. It is my truth and how I perceived my daily life; the personalities, physical descriptions of people who inhabited my world and helped form some of the opinions and beliefs that I possess until today. There are a few incidents recorded in this memoir that are interspersed with some figments of my imagination (that is usually quite vivid for a five-year-old).

The first years of my life began in Carrollton, Missouri, where I was born and lived with my father's relatives; most of them are deceased now. However, I located and started communicating with my only surviving first cousin, who is 90 years old, and quite sharp mentally. She spent considerable time with my paternal grandparents before their deaths and provided information about them to me. She proudly informed me her grandson was recently appointed Police Chief in St. Louis. Through her I have been in touch with second cousins I never knew.

After the Carrollton years, my memories are much more vivid, as they were spent with my maternal relatives. My only regret is that my mother and sisters are not still alive to help jog my memory on other facts that they remembered and I forgot or just left out. My youngest sister Marie, passed away September 19, 1992; my mother Benita, February 15, 1995; and my sister Mildred, March 19, 2001. My oldest sister Maxine, is still alive but is totally disabled as a result of contracting Alzheimer's Disease. One never realizes how much of a loss it is to lose all your siblings, leaving no one to reminisce with about those innocent childhood years.

Throughout these pages there may be stories that evoke a tear or two; some that may be hard to believe and others that will have you laughing out loud. Whatever emotions you experience while reading it, please know that it is an account of a life lived, one that the author is not ashamed of and is proud to have survived.

I make no claim to be an accomplished writer, but to the best of my ability, I have written this short memoir as accurately as possible, for my children, grandchildren and other family members or anyone else who might be interested.

I would like to acknowledge and extend a special thanks to people who were so giving of their time, patience and talent to this laborious, time-consuming task and without whose involvement, *Black Bananas* would not have been a book:

My first cousin (whom I mentioned previously), Izetta Cole, who is one of the sharpest 90-year-old ladies you'd ever want to know, and who still goes out periodically to listen to live modern jazz. Those many lengthy telephone conversations with her has endeared her so much to me, and I hope and pray I get to meet her before she is gone. May God continue to bless her. I love you Zett! Thank you.

Alice Leggett, a truly multi-talented lady (musically and artistically), who has become a dear friend and confidant since the inception of *Black Bananas*. She too, has devoted endless hours utilizing her amazing talent and knowledge as a graphic artist, organizing, editing and whipping this book into shape. Not to mention giving me a crash course in getting a book published. Her sense of humor, natural wit and unwavering belief that my book had merit has meant so much to me, I can't find words to express my appreciation. Alice, you are truly "The Wind Beneath My Wings!" Thank you.

Sandy, my wonderful wife, and number one fan, who gave me the title of "Star of The Bar" after we were married, and always said of me jokingly, "The boy's got potential!" She always believed in my ability to write my memoir and that it was a story worth telling. She never once complained when I would spend long, arduous hours in my "dungeon," missing meals she prepared for us to share together, but instead, mine were brought to the dungeon on a tray, becoming cold before being eaten. She took the time to read each re-write, and often wiping away tears, as she reflected on times and incidents that she lived through. As I have been told, a lesser person would have "kicked me to the curb!" I love you for loving me. Thank you.

Lastly, I would like to raise a toast to those who told me I would never complete this project; it was just another one of my foolish ideas that would never materialize. I sincerely thank all of you, because you became my biggest source of inspiration. Again, thank you!

-- Robert L. White

I dedicate this book
to my dearly loved Mother
who, unfortunately,
did not live to see
my efforts materialize.

BLACK BANANAS

The stock market crash that began in October of 1929 (Black Friday) was a major cause of the Depression. It sent the economy into a downward plunge and caused an abrupt end to wealth acquired through stock investments, and the good times and free-spending lifestyle of The Roaring Twenties. Millions of Americans who were accustomed to relative comfort and security, faced unemployment, handouts and soup lines. The national income dropped by 50 percent and unemployment rose to an estimated 25 percent of the labor force. Local newspapers constantly reported stories of Wall Street investors committing suicide by jumping from windows of high rise buildings. It was rumored hotel clerks would ask investors when they registered to rent a room, did they want it to sleep in or jump from. Picketing was rampant and whites now competed for jobs as elevator operators, busboys and janitors; jobs that were once regarded as "nigger tasks." It was also a fact that blacks were the last hired and first fired. African Americans entered the Depression long before the stock market crash and stayed there longer than any other Americans. By 1933, African Americans found it all but impossible to find jobs of any kind in agriculture or industry. As cotton prices dropped from eighteen cents per pound on the eve of the Depression to less than six cents per pound in 1933, some 12,000 black sharecroppers lost their precarious footing in southern agriculture and moved increasingly toward southern, northern and western cities. The proportion of blacks living in urban areas rose from 44 percent in 1930 to nearly 50 percent by the onset of World War II.

As the number of rural blacks seeking jobs in cities escalated, urban black workers experienced increasing difficulties. Urban unemployment reached over 50 percent, more than twice that of whites. In southern cities, white workers rallied around slogans such as, "No jobs for Niggers until every White Man has a job," and "Niggers, back to the cotton fields - city jobs are for white folks."

1

Since I did not have a say (as none of us do) about the circumstances surrounding my birth, such as when I would be born, where I would be born and to whom I would be born, I had to be content with the hand fate dealt me. If I would have had some control over it, I would have chosen not to be born black and to poor parents with only an elementary school education; during a time when segregation and discrimination against black people was commonplace throughout the country, especially in the midwest and south; nor in the midst of a depression, when everyone black and white, educated or not, was affected by it.

CARROLLTON, MISSOURI

So on Christmas Eve of 1929, in the small town of Carrollton, Missouri, I made my entrance at 12:58 P.M., weighing just over ten pounds; the second child of Herbert and Benita White. My mother was nineteen years old and my father thirty-one. To say they were elated over my arrival would be an exaggeration since they were victims of the Depression, poor and unemployed, and had another mouth to feed. My mother had a child, Maxine, a year and nine months older than me, when she married my father.

That was the first forgettable Christmas I would hand my parents. I was probably four years of age when my father and mother took

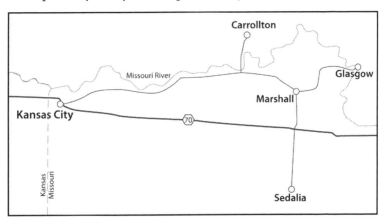

my two sisters and me to see Santa Claus. We got in line with the other parents and kids waiting our turn to sit on Santa's knee and tell him what we wanted for Christmas. When our turn came, my father picked me up and handed me toward Santa's outstretched arms. I took one look at this big, fat white man, with his long, white beard and started kicking, screaming and crying so loud, my dad reached out and pulled me back into his arms. I was so scared, I crapped my pants and all over dad's coat sleeve. Needless to say, that ended our visit with Santa.

From all official birth and death records I have been able to locate, and the few personal accounts I received, it appears that Carrollton is the pivotal town from which both my maternal and paternal relatives spent the early years raising their families. My father's eleven siblings (only six survived) were all born in Carrollton. Only my father and one of his sisters remained there all their lives. My mother's siblings, of which there were sixteen, were all born in Glasgow, Missouri and later moved to Carrollton. Once they became adults, they all left to live in other cities and states throughout the U.S. My grandparents then moved to Sedalia, Missouri where my grandfather opened a barbershop, and remained there the rest of their lives.

My paternal grandparents, Hezekiah and Eliza, also lived in Carrollton until their deaths and I have learned something of them over the years. My great-grandfather, named Robert, was a slave born in Moberly, Missouri (birth date unknown), evidently to a slave owner with the surname of White. Somewhere along the way, he ended up in Howard County, Missouri (city or town unknown). It was here he began a family, but no mention is made of a wife or the mother of his offspring. In 1832, my grandfather, Hezekiah was born. Two other children were born also, a brother named Albert and a sister (name unknown). It is not known if they were younger or older than Hezekiah. Nothing more is known of Albert or their sister. It is believed they were sold to another slave owner and their whereabouts unknown. After the Emancipation Proclamation was

Hezekiah White, my paternal grandfather.

Eliza Wiggins White, my paternal grandmother.

enacted, Hezekiah was freed, and reportedly enlisted in the Union Army. However, I have checked in the National Archives and searched the military records of the United States Colored Troops (USCT) for a Hezekiah White (the surname of his last known owner), who served during that period and was unable to find any records of him having served at all.

I learned recently from an older cousin who knew Hezekiah, and remembers hearing him speak often proudly of his Indian heritage. Judging from photos I have seen of him with his sharp features, white hair and beard, Indian mixture is a good possibility. There was no mention of any particular tribe.

Some time later, he met and married my grandmother, Eliza Wiggins, also born in Howard County, on June 1, 1859 to Adeline Quinn Wiggins. The name of her father is unknown. Eliza was just a young girl when he married her and she was treated as one of his children or his servant. Hezekiah was twenty-five years older than Eliza. In those days older men took young girls for their wives for the purpose of bearing many offspring. She was never allowed to address him as anything but Mr. White. Unfortunately, neither one of them attended school or were taught to read or write. Hezekiah made a living performing menial jobs and making and selling corn whiskey throughout the neighborhood. He died of prostate cancer on June 18, 1924. Coincidentally, Eliza died of tuberculosis of the hip on her birthday in 1926.

I knew my maternal grandparents very well since they both were alive when I was born and we visited them regularly. My grandfather, William (Bill, as he was called) Edward Yancey was born February 22, 1870 in Howard County (city or town unknown) Missouri. However, there is no known record of who his parents were. He met and married Georgia Henrietta Watts, fathering sixteen children; my mother was the eleventh.

My mother was born July 18, 1910 in the little farming town of Glasgow, Missouri, as I previously stated, and by the time she reached her teens, the family had moved to Carrollton. She was becoming rather wild and difficult to control; music and dancing was all she was interested in. Playing hooky from school was becoming

A young Bill Yancey, my maternal grandfather

Henrietta Watts Yancey, my maternal grandmother.

a constant occurrence with her and she was often found dancing to music outside beer joints and clubs since she was too young to go inside. She had earned a reputation with all her friends as being the best singer and dancer in the neighborhood and everyone marveled at her long, pretty legs. She got plenty of attention from the boys and she loved every bit of it. All new dances or songs that became popular, she would learn and teach her friends. One summer a traveling minstrel show was performing in little towns and communities throughout the area. The horse-drawn wagons traveled through the streets displaying a series of brightly-colored signs and pictures of the performers; bearded-ladies, knife-swallowers, fire-eaters, freaks of nature, clowns, magicians, singers and dancers. A barker, equipped with a megaphone and dressed in a cheap, well-worn tuxedo with tails and top hat, would work the people up by describing the acts, as a calliope played music in the background. Often one of the featured performers, such as a knife-swallower, would be brought out on stage for curious onlookers to see, enticing them to buy tickets to the show that would be performed in a large tent later that day.

My grandfather, Bill Yancey, in 1928 (Before I was born and before his barbering days).

My mother must have been very excited by all this and saw it as an opportunity to show off her talent and inquired about auditioning to join the troupe as a singer and dancer. They agreed and let her audition, singing a popular song of the era, "Bye-Bye Blackbird" while dancing the Charleston, a dance made popular during that period. Evidently she did quite well, because they hired her on the spot and she left with the minstrel troupe to perform in the neighboring town that same day.

As the day wore on, her father began questioning the other children as to her whereabouts. Unfortunately, she had mentioned to one of her sisters about her intentions to audition for the minstrel show, and told her father. He was absolutely furious and sent an older son to find her. After inquiring throughout the neighborhood, he was able to find out which town the minstrel was headed. Just before dark, he caught up with the minstrel and my mother. She was sitting on stage of the open trailer watching the act performing while waiting her turn. Her brother stood in the crowd watching also as they announced the next act. "And now, ladies and gentlemen, we present to you Miss Crazy Legs!" The music to "Bye-Bye Blackbird" began and she jumped up smiling and went into her act. The audience clapped to the beat and sang along with her while her long legs were flying as she danced from one end of the small stage to the other. Her brother walked up and positioned himself at one end of the stage, and when she danced over to where he was standing, he reached up, snatched her off stage and took her home. Mom's final appearance would be at home dancing to her father's music.

For Mom, it was one issue after another, and staying in school was the biggest. She was a bright student and very likeable but headstrong with her own agenda. At seventeen years of age, she had grown into a beautiful, tall and curvaceous olive-complexioned woman, possessing a bright smile which she was quick to display. Unfortunately, she was still very naive and innocent about life and the ways of the world. This innocence led to her becoming involved with a smooth-talking older guy, who promptly impregnated her and fled town immediately, dodging the wrath of her father and many brothers. After this incident her father became fed up and sent her back to Glasgow to live with her older sister, who was married with a family, but agreed to take her in temporarily until the baby was born. Her pregnancy was uncomplicated and on March 26, 1928, she gave birth to a healthy baby girl, naming her Maxine Ardell Woods, the surname of the father.

A year or so later, after returning to Carrollton with Baby Maxine, while attending church and singing in the choir she met a tall, thin, light-complexioned man with a wide, captivating smile, who also sang in the choir, named Herbert White. Although he was twelve years older, they were attracted to one another and after their initial meeting, he began courting her regularly. It wasn't long after that, he told her father he wanted to marry her. Of course my grandfather thought it was a great solution to the problem of having my mother and her young baby under foot. So my mother married my father and she and little Maxine moved out of her parents' house and into the home of Dad's sister, Lillian.

During the next five years my sisters Mildred and Marie were born. The three of us were born at home in a small bedroom (blacks could not be admitted to hospitals for any reason). It was a cramped room, dominated by an old iron-framed double bed in which all five of us slept. My father, when he was there, slept on a pallet on the floor. Except when we were outside playing, our time was spent in that room because we were not allowed to play or hang out in any other parts of the house. Mom would open the one window to air the room out, but since there was no screen on the window, flies and all sorts of bugs would swarm in. So, it was a case of open the window and the flies

Herbert White, my father, born May 4, 1898. (The only existing picture of him)

swarm in, close the window and you are sweating again. In the winter she put rags around the door and window frame to help keep the cold out.

My Aunt Lillian's (we called her Aunt Lin) home had three bedrooms, a living room (she called the parlor) and a kitchen. The house was always dark. No window shades or doors were ever opened. She said this kept the house cool. In the living room sat an old upright piano which she swore she was going to learn to play one of these days, an ornate, dark blue velvet-covered couch which no one was permitted to sit on. It was "for company" that never came. The outside of the house had been painted white once upon a time but now, the paint was peeling off the weather-beaten wood. The front porch was supported by round wooden pillars on each side. Off to one side of the dilapidated porch was a big, faded grey wicker rocking chair with a worn out cushion, in which Aunt Lin would sit during summer days rocking and humming old Negro spirituals that were passed down from slavery days. The songs all spoke of "finally being free and laying these tired old bones down to rest," "going home to Jesus to walk the streets of gold," "getting wings and shouting all over God's heaven." An unkempt,

Mildred, Maxine and Robert.

9

overgrown lawn, divided by a small pathway led out to a gravel-covered street, that crunched loudly as vehicles drove over it. In the rear of the house was a large, would-be backyard area where burnt coal cinders from the stoves used for heating and cooking were scattered. Off to one side, was a wooden shed with a corrugated tin roof that may have been used as a tool storage shed but now filled with odds and ends, broken furniture and trash. Behind the shed was a fenced off portion where once a vegetable garden grew, now filled with dried-up corn stalks and tall weeds . Aunt Lin told me how the garden used to produce the biggest and juiciest tomatoes you ever tasted and she was going to start planting them again one day. The weather-beaten outhouse sat opposite the would-be garden area. I played amongst these weeds against my mothers' warnings to stay out, for fear of being bitten by a snake. This was my private jungle and my imagination ran rampant. One day I was playing in my jungle while eating a piece of bread when suddenly two big, white roosters came out of nowhere, flew upon my head and started pecking my hands as they took my bread away from me. I ran out of there and into the house crying for my mother with blood dripping on the linoleum covered kitchen floor.

My memories of Carrollton are fairly limited since I was quite young and we only lived there for about five years but, there is one rather sad memory I hold onto. I met a boy who lived a few doors up the street from us. His name was Ralph Martin and we played together everyday. He was much larger than me (of course every-one was, I was small for my age and stayed that way throughout high school) and a little older, so I looked up to him. If he said do it, I did it. One day Ralph and I and my new black and white puppy Pee-Wee were walking along a creek that was located on the edge of town. My father had just brought Pee Wee home for me a few days earlier. Ralph told me that all dogs knew how to swim natu-rally and didn't need to be taught. I said to him, "Not puppies!" And he told me, "Yes, even puppies! Let me show you!" He picked Pee-Wee up and threw him into the creek. Pee Wee started yelping and struggling to swim and keep his head above the murky brown water, then finally, his head went under and he never came back up. I starting crying uncontrollably and ran home as fast as I could to tell my parents what had happened. My father went immediately to Ralph's house and told his mother what he had done. She apologized, telling us how sorry she was, then tore into Ralph with such anger and rage. She beat him so long and hard, until I began to feel sorry for him. Ralph didn't come around much after that. I found out later the reason he drowned my puppy was, he was jealous because his parents wouldn't let him have one.

My Dad worked at an ice cream confectionery and brought ice cream home regularly, although he didn't like ice cream. I remember my sisters and I would sit on the front porch around Aunt Lin's big wicker chair, eating ice cream and listening to her rocking and talking about all the big things she was going to do when her "ship came in." My mother called what she was doing, "Building Air Castles." Everything she talked about doing such as, learning to play the piano, planting a vegetable garden or whatever was always prefaced by, "One day." It was all she could do to get up from the chair she was sitting in. Those pleasant times came to an end when my father got laid off and couldn't find work anywhere. At night I would listen to my mother and father arguing very loudly about money. I always expected my father to physically abuse my mother, but he never did. My father was not that kind of man. He would just curse and yell, then walk out slamming the door and return hours later drunk. Aunt Lin started complaining about all of us living off of her and blamed my mother for having so many kids and no way to take care of them. Never once did she put any of the blame on my father. Mom became fed up with my father's drunken ways and Aunt Lin's complaining, so she started looking for work and eventually found work as a maid in the homes of white families. Aunt Lin told Mom she needed to find someone to care for us while she worked because she was not going to do it. Somehow Mom was referred to a lady nearby who would be willing to take care of us.

The first day Mom took us to her house, we were introduced to her as Mrs. Washington but she corrected Mom and said, "Call me Washie, everyone does!" Washie was a very thin, older woman, who had difficulty walking. She looked to be Caucasian, but spoke with a black accent. Her skin was wrinkled with thin, blue veins running up and down her hands and arms. She had long, straight grey hair which she wore in a loose bun on the back of her head. I noticed a full set of upper and lower false teeth sitting in a glass of water

Me, at 5 years old.

on a night stand beside her bed. Without her teeth in, it caused her cheeks to sink in and her long narrow chin to jut out farther. She reminded me of the witch that is depicted riding a broom through the skies on Halloween. I was somewhat afraid of her and did not like her from our first meeting and had more reason to dislike her after we started staying with her. The house was overcrowded with junky old furniture and it smelled of urine, due to a big round blue and white ceramic night chamber with a matching lid that sat in the middle of the room. We often witnessed her using the pot openly in front of us. She would sit bent over urinating, while hitting herself with her fist in the kidney area. Mom told us this was because she had a kidney problem and it helped her urinate.

We were dropped off at her house and she fixed our breakfast which usually consisted of oatmeal or Cream of Wheat, both of which were served to us lumpy and barely warm. When she thought it was too hot, she would test it by taking a spoon-full into her mouth, spitting it back into the spoon and feeding it to us. I

Maxine, age 7 years old.

would have no part of that and told her so. She would become angry, hitting me with the back of the spoon and forcing me to eat it. I complained to Mom about it so much so, that she began bringing a box of corn flakes, powdered sugar and a can of Carnation Evaporated Milk, which we diluted with water to make it go farther, for our breakfasts. Then for lunch, she had made us peanut butter and jelly sandwiches.

The good times we had at home were becoming less frequent, due to arguments between my mother, father and Aunt Lin. Aunt Lin's grown son Wayman (everyone called "Bubba"), who was about the same age as my father, lived in the house also with no job. He and my father were drinking buddies and stayed drunk most of the time. The times when they were sober, they were trying to figure out where the next drink would come from. Mom would take the vanilla extract off the kitchen shelf and hide it to keep them from drinking it, when they could not find money to buy booze. Aunt Lin's only income was her late husband's military pension and she was much too lazy and overweight to hold a job. The domestic work my mother was doing did not pay enough for us to move out and into a place of our own. So there were a total of eight of us living in this small house and tension began to build. Sometimes my father would steal what little money mom had put away for food and buy booze, leaving us with only small amounts of food, or none at all.

Aunt Lin was nice enough to us kids at first, but she disliked my

Benita White, my mother.

mother for some reason we never knew and she became intolerant of us. It could have been because my mother had my oldest sister when she and my father married and she thought Mom was taking advantage of her brother. Who knows for sure. However, it got so bad that she kicked Mom and the four of us out of the house. We stayed in the old corrugated tin shed in the back yard sleeping on a discarded and dirty double mattress, covering up with two ragged army blankets for about three weeks. Thank God it was summer. There was an old wood burning cook stove in the back yard that my Mother cleaned up and started cooking on. I remember her cooking oatmeal and frying corn cakes on it. Most of the time she would bring home leftovers from the homes where she had worked that day. I thought, as I ate some of this left-over food, how good it tasted and white people ate such good food. Many nights my mother never ate anything, what there was she gave to us. My father did nothing to help. His only concern was getting his next drink. Many nights when I was lying on the mattress, supposedly sleeping, I would watch my mother standing in the corner of the shed crying. I felt sorry for her and lay there crying quietly also.

This continued for several weeks until another one of my father's sisters, Roberta, living in Detroit, Michigan came to Carrollton for a visit and saw the situation and felt sorry for us. Roberta, whom we called Aunt Rob, was a grammar-school teacher in Detroit, married with no children, but took a great liking to us, especially me, since I was named after her and my great-grandfather. Well, Aunt Rob contacted another of her sisters, Bertha, who lived close by in Marshall, Missouri. She told her of our situation and asked if she would help by allowing us to live with her. Aunt Rob said she would send some money each month to help out. She readily agreed, and that was the beginning of the end of my parents' marriage when we packed up and moved to Marshall, Missouri.

I learned later that Aunt Lin's son, Bubba, fell asleep while drunk one night and burned the house down. Fortunately, no one was injured.

MARSHALL, MISSOURI

Marshall is another small farming town located twenty-five miles from Carrollton, the governing seat of Saline County, nestled between Branson and the skylines of Kansas City. Most civic and commercial activity was centered around the old town square where locals sat daily on wooden benches in the court house yard whittling, chewing tobacco and the fat. The town folk looked forward to the annual corn-husking contest that was held every summer. Contestants from surrounding farms would compete to win a big blue ribbon and have their picture run in the local and neighboring town newspapers. They became local celebrities for that year. Like all of Missouri at the time, Marshall was completely segregated. Colored people lived in the east end of town, with unpaved streets and no sidewalks and white people lived throughout the rest of the town. The street in front of our little two-storied brick school was paved with asphalt right up to where the school grounds ended. After that, nothing but dirt, that turned into ankle-deep mud when it rained or snowed.

I was six years old when we moved in with our Aunt Bertha, whom we affectionately started calling Aunt Boo. She and her husband (I seriously doubt if they were legally married), Uncle Louis, lived in a small, three-roomed house with an outdoor toilet in the back yard which she was unable to use because of her obesity and inability to walk any distance. My sister Mildred and I would imitate her as she got up to start walking. She would sit there holding on to the arms of the chair grunting and groaning as she rocked back and forth two or three times, to pick up momentum. When she finally got enough motion going, she would come forward with her head and upper body bent over so far it appeared as though she were going to topple over on the floor headfirst. Then her big body would come out of the chair in a bent over position, taking a few small off-balance steps before she finally straightened up. We would do it along with her. Looking back, it was a bit cruel to imitate her but, she would laugh right along with us. She was a big-boned, obese, caramel complexioned woman who possessed a warm and friendly personality and was quick to flash a big, two-toothed smile, followed by a loud cackling laugh causing her belly to shake like a big bowl of Jell-O. Her sense of humor picked up even more so, when she and Uncle Louis would do their monthly drinking after he received his government disability check for having been gassed in World War I.

She was so big that a chair was made especially for her; in the middle was a big round hole, cut out and covered with a plywood board and a pillow when not being used as her toilet. Underneath, a huge bucket was placed to catch the urine and excrement. Uncle Louis had the responsibility of carrying the bucket to the outhouse each morning. In that small house, it was never taken out soon enough! The smell built up overnight and was nearly intolerable, especially in the hot and humid summer months. Unfortunately, when Uncle Louis was on a drunken binge and not at home, my sister Maxine or I had to carry it out and empty it in the outhouse. Aunt Boo's days were spent going from the bed (which the chair sat next to), to the chair and to the kitchen. The only time she left the house was to go to the front porch to cool off, if the flies and mosquitoes were not too bothersome. She made her own dresses out of old cloth flour sacks she ripped open and sewed together with the brand name still visible. I can still see the blue "Maude S Flour" name on all her dresses.

Uncle Louis was a dark-complexioned, balding, slender man of medium height with large bulging eyes that were bloodshot most of the time. He was an even-tempered man, rather soft spoken and never complained about Aunt Boo constantly bossing him around. He suffered from epileptic seizures he claimed were caused from having been gassed in World War I, while fighting in France. He would fall out on the floor, shaking violently, his eyes rolled back in his head while frothing at the mouth. Aunt Boo would have us sit on him to help hold him still while she reached into his mouth, pulling his tongue out and putting a pencil under it. She said this was necessary to keep him from choking to death on his tongue.

The seizures usually lasted for about ten to twenty minutes.

Oddly, they seemed to occur shortly after he received his monthly check and was coming off of a two or three day drunken binge. Aunt Boo would curse him, calling him a "No good worthless drunk!" He'd just sit, rubbing his bald head with his big red tear-filled eyes darting back and forth over the ceiling, then pleadingly say, "Now Bertie, don't be so mean to me!" Actually, her main gripe was he would cash his check and get drunk before she got her hands on the money to issue him what she wanted him to spend. Of course, now he would have to go buy her some booze so she could drink her share. My sister Mildred and I loved this time of the month because she was always very generous with her money and would give us a quarter or so for performing some little song or doing something to make her laugh. Whenever she misplaced her purse, which was often when she drank, we would find it and then help ourselves to a little extra money. She never realized it was gone.

By now, I was about seven years old and we had settled in to life in Marshall pretty good. Mom was finding work here and there and my sisters and I had made friends in the neighborhood and at school. Aunt Boo made us welcome in her little three-room house. We were happy, despite our cramped living quarters. Aunt Boo and Uncle Louis slept in the living room in a big, crudely made wooden bed. The room also had a old potbellied stove against one wall. My mother and sisters slept in the small bedroom on an old iron double bed. I had a pallet on the floor. The walls and ceilings in both rooms had been papered at some time in the past but now most of it was loose, cracked and peeling off, due mainly to the heat, creating all types of odd patterns on the walls. My sisters and I would make a game out of looking at the shapes while laying in bed and visualize all sorts of images and animals.

Uncle Louis had a part-time job working on a trash truck that collected rubbish from mostly markets and restaurants. They collected a lot of boxes and cartons that fruits and vegetables were packed in and delivered to the markets, as well as assorted pastries and lunchmeats. When new deliveries were made, the older items were taken off the shelves and discarded. A lot of the items that were thrown out were not totally rotten, just not fresh enough to be on display. The trash truck collected all of these soiled food items, along with other trash and took it to the dumping area which was, fortunately, located directly behind our house.

When the truck had finished unloading and drove away, my sisters and I would climb over the small wire fence and were right in the middle of all those slightly dirty and soiled goodies! We collected donuts and other pastries after brushing off coffee grounds and other grit and grime and began eating them on the spot. Apples, oranges, peaches, grapes, bananas and any other fruit you can name was there for us. Usually the fruit had a rotten spot on it, but the rest of it was perfectly good. We would stick our finger down into the rotten spot, twirl it around the rotten spot, thereby collecting all the rot on our finger, then sling it to the ground and begin eating the fruit. Bananas were very soft and brown or black, but we ate them after pinching off the very soft part on the end, while shooing away the little fruit flies. During this time I had not eaten a yellow banana.

What we did not eat there, we took home other items, such as bread, lunchmeat, potatoes, tomatoes, onions, lettuce and other slightly soiled vegetables. Aunt Boo would wash them with soap and water, and it ultimately ended up on our plates for dinner or in our lunch bags.

Other kids would come to the dump with their parents carrying gunny-sacks (burlap bags) to gather what they could also. Luckily, we had first pick because we knew the days Uncle Louis would be working on the truck. So when they got there, the best of the pickings were gone.

Aunt Boo had taken over the job of preparing our lunches for school because Mom would leave for work before we got up for school. It consisted of the washed lunchmeats and partially rotted fruit, sometimes packed in brown bags, other times wrapped in newspaper and tied with a string.

My sister Mildred and I were in the same classroom, as each classroom housed two grades. I was in the second grade and she was in the first. One day we came in, took our assigned seats and the teacher, Mrs. Willa Brown began calling the attendance roll.

Upon completion, she assigned work for us to do. As we worked, she strolled slowly around the room glancing at each of us approvingly. When she reached my desk, she stopped and began sniffing noticeably, then picked up my lunch bag, sniffed it and started frowning. With her nose still turned up, she picked up my lunch and walked straight to the trash can. Afterwards, she went to Mildred's desk and did the same thing. With Mildred in tow, she returned to my desk and asked me, quietly, to follow her into the cloak room. She closed the door and very softly, and somewhat sadly, informed us our lunches were rotten and not safe to eat. She said, "Today, I am buying your lunches in the cafeteria." Evidently, Maxine experienced the same thing too, because we saw her there eating, too. Mrs. Brown told Mom about it and we never brought any Dump Food to school again. But it did not stop us from our regular Dump Digging. We were back at it the next time the truck came.

Even today, I have to stop and think before throwing away an apple with a rotten spot on it. I always think, "It's only one little spot! I could finger that out and the rest of the apple would be good." I'm still somewhat attracted to bananas that are a little soft and brown, but I restrain myself. Still seems a little wasteful to me.

In Missouri, at that time, front porches were used regularly on summer evenings. Some had swings on them, which was a joy for children and older people alike. Although our porch did not have one, there were several chairs that the adults sat in and we sat around on the grass or edges of the porch, jumping up and down chasing fireflies (lightning bugs). My sisters would catch them, pull off their glowing tails and place them on their ear lobes for earrings or rings for their fingers.

Our front porch was also used for sing-a-longs. Everyone would join in. Aunt Boo and Uncle Louis were especially involved when they had been drinking and in a happy mood. Aunt Boo had a very good contralto voice and knew harmony perfectly. She gave everyone their parts. My mother, three sisters, Uncle Louis and I, all singing in harmony, songs ranging from Negro Spirituals to the popular songs of the day. Sometimes neighbors would come over and join in. These were very good times regardless of being dirt poor.

Other times the porch was filled with people, mostly men with their Home Brewed Beer and White Lightning whiskey, gathered around our little table top radio listening to Joe Louis' heavyweight fights. You never heard such cussing, yelling and complaining when the radio had brief periods of static during the fight, blocking out the fight. Especially when it seemed Joe Louis was getting beat up pretty badly and losing the fight.

It was June 22, 1938, I was nine years old and it was my first time listening to a Joe Louis Championship fight. Joe Louis was having a return match with Max Schmeling, the German heavyweight boxer, who had beaten Joe Louis in a previous match and had taken the title away from him. Everyone kept talking about the Germans being Nazis and how they thought they were superior to Americans, especially low-classed Black People.

Two years earlier, during the 1936 Summer Olympic Games held in Berlin, Germany, Jesse Owens was the first black American track and field athlete to win four gold medals; one in the 100 meters, one in the 200 meters, one in the long jump and the last one in the 4x100 meters relay. Hitler was annoyed with this black man, calling him part animal, out of the jungle and refused to shake his hand on the winners' podium. So Germans were not thought of very highly by Americans during this time. Jesse Owens had beat the Germans and now it was Joe Louis' turn to whip Schmeling once and for all, and be crowned The World's Heavyweight Champion!

Round one began and so did the excitement on our porch. As each round progressed, I was up, throwing punches in the air as if I were helping Joe Louis whip Schmeling. When the fight was finally over and Joe Louis had knocked him out cold, you never heard such whooping and hollering, jumping up and down all over the porch and yard. You could hear people doing the same thing throughout the neighborhood. Car horns were blaring up and down the streets. Beer joints, barbecue shacks and the few black cafes that existed were doing a lot of business for the rest of the night.

Joe Louis was the only black internationally known personality who was accepted and respected by black and white people alike. He was declared "Everybody's Champion." "The Brown Bomber," as he was affectionately nicknamed, was interviewed after the fight and was asked how he felt about the fight. He said he was a little confused. When asked why, he replied, "I was hitting him so hard, I had to go around behind him to see what was holding him up!"

We black people had well-known musicians in those days, such as; Louie Armstrong, Duke Ellington, Count Basie, Cab Calloway and many others, but they did not garner the international respect of Joe Louis. Jesse Owens was well thought of also but, we didn't hear of him after the Olympics. Then there were black baseball players who were well known throughout the black communities; Satchel Paige, Josh Gibson and a few others who played on the Negro teams that barnstormed throughout the mid-west and southern states, but were not nationally known because of segregation. Consequently, us young black boys never aspired to be like them, but we all wanted to be Joe Louis.

The company that makes Wheaties, the breakfast cereal, had a slogan, "Wheaties! The Breakfast of Champions!" Well, naturally I insisted we buy that brand of cereal. Each morning I had the box in front of me as I ate my breakfast, believing every word of the advertisement. Whenever a picture was taken of me, I always

"Joe Louis," wearing "relief" issued coveralls, with Marie and Mildred.

struck a boxing stance with my fists balled up. What made matters worse, local men told me I would be a good boxer because I was a Southpaw. I never knew what a southpaw was, but I took it to mean I was something special.

We were very poor, but we didn't know it. There was nothing to compare our life to. It was all we knew. We were no worse off than all the other families in the neighborhood. Everyone was on relief (welfare) with one parent raising the family, usually the mother. I knew of very few friends who had a father living with them. When, and if they did show up, it was only briefly and they would leave again. Shortly thereafter, the mother would give birth to another child to raise alone. I felt no shame when I had to put cardboard in my shoes to keep my feet dry from the snow and rain and pull my socks forward, tucking them under my toes, so as to hide the big hole in the heel. Everyone did it. We weren't poor, we were "Po!"

By the time I reached the third grade, we moved out of Aunt Boo's house and into our own little house, down the road a piece from Aunt Boo. It was a two-roomer, a small kitchen with a wood burning stove for cooking and a room that doubled as a living room and bedroom. A little pot-bellied stove stood off to one side of the room with its round, black stove pipe that reached the ceiling and out through the roof, expelling the smoke from the coal and wood we burned in it. Mom brought our old iron double bed and placed it against one wall. I resumed my usual sleeping place, on a pallet made on the floor next to the stove. On winter nights, I stayed good and warm until the coals burned out in the early morning hours.

The kitchen had old worn, cracked linoleum tacked to the floor, and in the living/bedroom, there was threadbare carpeting, so worn the pattern was gone and the threads were visible. Underneath were old, gray, washed out floorboards, that when you jumped or walked heavily on them, you would see small puffs of dust rise up. Mom constantly sprinkled water on the carpet when she swept to keep the dust down.

Fortunately, the house had electricity, so we had little to no use for our kerosene lamps any longer. In the middle of the kitchen and living room ceilings was a long electric wire that hung down with a light bulb attached to it. We loved it! Electricity, yes! Plumbing, no! We still had our two-holed outhouse in the backyard.

Yancey Family Reunion in Sedalia, Missouri, circa 1937. Maxine, me, Marie and Mildred sitting in front row; Mom standing fifth from the right in white dress.

We had to get our water from a neighbor's faucet outside his house, a block or so down the road. It became Maxine's and my job to take a galvanized bucket and get the water when it was needed, a job we both hated. I can still feel the pain from that wire handle cutting into the palm of my hand as we trudged back up the road with this bucket of water. We would trade off carrying it after so many steps. By the time we got home, the bucket was three-quarters full which meant we would have to return to refill it sooner. It was used for drinking, cooking, washing dishes and washing our faces and hands.

We had a tin pan called the washing pan for washing faces and hands; and a dish pan for doing the dishes. Then for drinking, we had a big tin dipper that we would dip into the bucket, fill up and pour into a tin cup or a jelly drinking jar. We dreaded Saturdays the most because we had to make so many trips to fill up the tin tub for taking our baths and be ready for church on Sunday morning. Heating the water on the stove for those baths took forever.

On Aunt Boo's little table top radio, Maxine and I used to listen to the music being broadcast. We would sing along with the popular singers of the day, Bing Crosby, Frank Sinatra, Eddie Arnold, Gene Autry and The Sons of The Pioneers. Our favorite was Frank Sinatra; we knew all of his songs. I had seen him singing in a movie we attended.

Afterwards, I came home and pretended to be him. I stood on a chair in front of the single electric light dangling in the center of the room and started singing, using the light bulb as my microphone and spotlight. When I finished, my sisters would applaud and swoon.

Mom had signed up for the Federal Emergency Relief Program which President Franklin Delano Roosevelt had put into law to provide food and clothing for needy families. Once a month Mom and I would take our burlap bag and stand in the long lines with the other people, outside a government building, waiting to receive food. I remember wearing relief issued clothing; gray, pin-striped overalls and a drab blue one-pieced jump-suit to school alongside other kids who wore the same clothing. Seemingly, everyone was on relief or had someone who was employed by the WPA (Work Projects Administration), another government run program that built bridges, parks and schools throughout the state. Men were sent away for months working on these projects. Women working with the WPA were taught to use sewing machines and employed making the clothing that was to be distributed. Statistics had proven that 60% of African American women in Missouri were single parents and receiving aid from the Relief Program or the Works Projects Administration.

Mom eventually found steady work as a maid or cook in wealthy white homes, but never made enough to cover our needs, so she found extra work doing whatever she could find to fill the need. Sometimes she would bring home bundles of clothing from the families she cooked or cleaned for, to be ironed. We had no electric iron, only small irons made of cast iron that had to be heated on our coal-burning stove. She would put two or three of them on the top of the stove until they were hot and use each one until they cooled off, then repeat the process until she had completed ironing all the clothes. I remember her being up late at night ironing. Sometimes I would ask if I could stay up and keep her company while she ironed. She agreed and I would sit on the floor by the ironing board and ask her a million questions until she got tired of my endless questions and tell me to shut up and go to bed. Other times I would tell her, "When I grow up, I am going to make a lot of money and take care of you and you'll never have to work anymore."

One summer Mom told me I would be going to work with her, because the lady for whom she was working needed someone to do a little cleaning up in the yard and Mom told her that I could do the work. I thought, this was just great! I felt important because I had a job and was getting paid! Naturally, I couldn't wait to brag to my buddies about it, knowing they would envy me.

I got up early the next day with my mother, ate a bowl of cereal and off we went to work. Marshall had no public transportation and we had no car, so we walked. We arrived at this big, white house with a neatly trimmed lawn and a long concrete driveway that ran alongside the length of the house, ending at the garage which was larger than the house we lived in. Attached to the front of the house was a big covered porch with a swing on it. I was very impressed. As I followed Mom down the driveway towards the rear of the house, I asked if we were going to the garage. She answered, "No Boy, we do not enter through the front door, the servants' entrance is through the back door; remember that!"

We entered into a large kitchen painted white and trimmed in red. It was so spotless you could eat off of the floor. The stove was gas and all the knobs were trimmed in red. In the ceiling were electric lights and in one corner was a big white oval shaped box with the word "Frigidaire" written on the door. I found out shortly, it was the ice box. It was the first one I had ever seen. At home we had a small wooden icebox with a door that opened up and held a twenty-five pound chunk of ice and everything that was to be kept cold was put in a lower compartment on the bottom.

Mom greeted the lady who had entered the kitchen, then introduced me. "Mrs. Henley, this is my son Robert, who is ready to do the yard work you needed done." She turned and looked at me pleasantly and said, "Well hello young man! Do you think you are ready for a day's work?" "Yes Ma'am," I quickly replied. She then said, "Good, come with me!" And I followed this tall, slender woman with light brown hair out the back door, down the driveway, leaving my mother standing in the kitchen. We stopped at the front porch where she picked up a cardboard box and handed it to me. In it were a pair of gardening shears. She then asked, "Now Robert, I want you to trim all the tall grass around the edges of the sidewalk and down the driveway. Do you think you can manage that?" I assured her I could do it as she smiled and said, "Good, I'll call you for lunch when it's time!" I thought, "Wow, I get lunch and get paid too!" I started in right away clipping the grass, putting it into the box and thinking about how much money she would give me when I was through and how I would spend it.

Time passed quickly and before I knew it, Mrs. Henley told me to stop working and come up on the porch, it was time for lunch. By the time I reached the porch, I saw my mother coming through the door carrying a small tray with a sandwich and several cookies on it, and a big glass of lemonade with small rectangular pieces of ice in it, not chunks of ice like we had at home. This was my first time seeing ice cubes. She sat it down at the top of the steps. When I was approaching the steps, I had noticed a young, blonde, green-eyed girl a bit younger than me, sitting and swinging quietly on the swing staring at me continuously. I sat to eat my lunch and noticed she was eating a sandwich also and drinking a glass of milk. Mom turned to the girl and said, "Mary Ann, this is my son, Robert, and this is Mary Ann, Robert, Mrs. Henley's daughter. Your mother wanted me to bring Robert to do some yard work for her today!" I nodded and gave her a small grin then continued eating. She still just stared. Mom told me when I had finished my lunch she would be out to pick up the tray.

Mary Ann's constant, puzzling stare was causing me to wonder if she had some mental problems and I was starting to feel some-what sorry for her. Just as I had finished my lunch, I noticed her starting to walk towards me with a quizzical smile on her face. When she reached where I was sitting, she looked down at me and said, "Robert, would you mind if I asked you a personal question?" Completely stunned, I turned to face her and said, "No, I don't think I would mind, what is it?"

Hesitantly, she started speaking, "Well, why are you so dirty, do you ever take a bath?" I replied, "I am not dirty, and I take a bath every Saturday night!" Still confused, she continued, "Well, why does your skin look so dark and dirty? Is it that color all over your body? I explained to her my skin was the same color all over my body, it's just the color of my skin. She seemed to accept my explanation and then asked if she could touch me. I agreed as she reached out and gently rubbed my arm. Smilingly, she said, "Oh! So without your clothes, you look like the gingerbread man, huh?" I was left speechless just staring at her.

When I finished my work for the day, Mrs. Henley thanked me and handed me a crisp, new dollar bill. I smiled, thanked her and put the dollar bill in my pocket immediately. As Mom and I walked home, I kept my hand in my pocket holding onto that dollar bill to be sure it did not, mysteriously jump out of my pocket and fly away. Thoughts of what I would spend it on kept spinning in my head constantly. Along the way I told Mom about my encounter with Mary Ann. When I had completed my story, Mom burst out laughing so hard, tears rolled down her face. I didn't quite see the humor. When we arrived at home, she told the story to my sisters and they too, started laughing just as hard as Mom. Jokingly, they called me Gingerbread Man for quite some time afterwards.

As far as I can remember, Bill Yancey supported his family by operating his own barber shop and tending a large garden at home where he grew most of the vegetables to feed his many children. Henrietta (everyone called her Etta) was a housewife and spent a lot of her time as a midwife helping to deliver babies. Both possessed at least an elementary school education and kept abreast of the current events of the day by listening to the evening news on their little table-top radio and reading the newspaper daily. I can still picture Grandpa sitting at the kitchen table after breakfast, reading the newspaper, lifting his cup of hot coffee from the saucer, then slowly pouring it back into the saucer and gently blowing on it to cool it, before sipping.

They made a rather pleasant looking couple; he was a tall, thin, dark brown-skinned man, with chiseled features. His head was bald except around the edges. My grandmother was a very light-complexioned woman of medium height and weight, with very fine grey hair and sharp features. Her white racial mixture was evident but it was never discussed. It is rumored one of her brothers left home as a young man, lived his life as a white man and never contacted the family again.

Several summers I spent with my grandparents in Sedalia, Missouri. Some days, my grandfather would take me to his barbershop with him where I would earn a dollar or two shining the shoes of his customers. When he paid me at the end of the day, he'd place coin after coin in my hand saying, "Honest pay for an honest day's work, remember that, son!" I also remember how he and one or two of his customers would take trips to a room in the rear of the shop, looking over their shoulders warily as they went, then reappear, clearing their throats and wiping their mouths. I was aware that my grandfather kept a little flask of liquor in his inner coat pocket because I had sneaked into the back room, pulled the shiny metal container out and took a big sniff of it. He was a well-respected man around Sedalia; always dressed in a three-piece suit, a heavily-starched white shirt, and tie. On each shirt sleeve at the elbow he wore what appeared to be, elastic garters. He wore his pants trussed up high with suspenders and a belt. I never understood the reasoning for wearing both. Underneath his clothing he wore long johns underwear with the legs tucked in his black socks, held up by garters also. His shoes were black high tops, polished so highly, you could see your reflection in the toes. He topped it all off with a nicely creased fedora, giving the appearance of a successful middle-class business man. Grandpa was a pleasant man with a slight sense of humor and I liked being around him. With him, I got that fatherly image that was sorely lacking in my life. When we walked home at the end of the day, I was always impressed with the way passers-by, black or white, would address him as Mr. Yancey. The respect he received was just the opposite of how my father was treated. When passing ladies, he would smile pleasantly, tip his hat and politely speak to them. It's a possibility the few nips of booze he had taken throughout the course of the day, helped put a spring in his step and brighten his overall demeanor a bit. Regardless, I admired him and his gentlemanly demeanor. He passed away April 18, 1947 from a chronic kidney disease.

My grandmother was not as personable. She was a stern taskmaster, very serious with no sense of humor. After having sixteen children, I don't think anyone would have found very much funny. I was somewhat afraid of her and steered cleared of her as much as possible. I never cared much for her cooking, and even less after walking into her bedroom one night, and seeing a complete set of upper and lower false teeth smiling at me in a glass of water, like I had seen earlier in Carrollton with our baby sitter Washie. For some reason, I thought of them each time we sat down to eat, causing my appetite to disappear. Fortunately, she was out of the house a lot helping deliver babies and to my delight, either my mother or one of her sisters did most of the cooking.

Grandma suffered from diabetes and during the early summer months of 1942, became seriously ill; needing someone to care for her. Since we lived the closest, only thirty miles away, Mom loaded us up and off we went to stay with her for awhile. During our stay, her doctor revealed the diabetes had progressed to the stage where he would have to remove her big toe. The operation was performed at home one afternoon. After the removal, he wrapped the toe in gauze, then newspaper and carried it to the back yard, dumping it in the trash barrel to be burned later. I was playing in the backyard and observed him put the toe in the trash. For some reason, my curiosity was aroused as I watched the disposal take place. I had to see that toe. Once the doctor went back inside the house, I went over to the container and picked up the wrapped paper package. Carefully, I began unwrapping it, exposing this bloody toe. It had the terrible odor of dead and rotting flesh and had turned a blackish-blue color, covered with dark red blood, some parts still wet, other parts clotted. I fought off the urge to vomit as I quickly rewrapped it and threw it back in the trash. To this day, I have no idea what compelled me to do something so grossly unpleasant.

My grandmother's diabetes was the cause of her death that summer. She passed away on August 26, 1942.

We attended the North Street Methodist Church where Mom sang in the choir. She still had her beautiful second soprano voice and was a favorite soloist in the choir. I can still see her on the front row of the choir singing, yet giving us the evil eye if we were misbehaving out in the audience. I never understood how she could keep singing and give us a look that said, "I'm going to whip your butts

Maxine, Mom, Marie, me and Mildred

if you don't stop acting a fool." More often than not, it was me.

I remember one Easter, we were all at church wearing our new Easter outfits. Mom had bought us all new Easter clothes. I had a nice double-breasted brown suit, brown striped tie and a nicely creased brown hat. I felt very special that day. We walked into church, took our usual seats where Mom could see us from the choir box. I sat down next to my sisters, putting my hat on the seat beside me. Shortly thereafter, other people started filing in to take seats on our row. Before I knew it, a big fat woman came into our row, and without as much as a glance, sat her big, fat butt down on my brand new hat, crushing it flat! She leaned to one side and pulled my flattened hat out, smiled at me and said something that sounded like an apology, but I was too mad to hear what she said. Of course, Mom said I should have held it in my hand like most men do. I never wore a hat to church again.

I was getting older, but was not growing much. My popularity grew because I could draw mostly anything. My friends always asked me to draw cowboys for them or some superhero out of comic books or the comic section of the Sunday newspaper.

My teacher also knew I could draw and would excuse me from doing schoolwork to come up front and draw holidays scenes on the blackboard with colored chalk for each holiday season. I drew Santa with a bag full of toys for the Christmas season, a witch riding through the skies on a broom for Halloween and a big, fat multi-colored turkey on Thanksgiving. Naturally, I milked it for all it was worth to get out of doing the school work. I would look back at my friends and laugh at them as they worked away doing boring math problems or something equally as boring.

Our little school was a two-storied red-bricked building that housed grades kindergarten through the ninth year. Upon completion of the ninth grade, students had to be bused to Sedalia, a town twenty-nine miles away to attend high school since Marshall did not have one. This resulted in many children concluding their education at the ninth grade and finding work on farms and other non-skilled jobs in Marshall.

By the time I entered the fourth grade, the school had hired a new principal to run the school. His name was Professor G.E. Lansdowne, a handsome, young, light-brown skinned man who had recently graduated from college with a Masters Degree in Education.

He was very interested in athletics and had excelled in track and field himself while in college. Needless to say, he instituted a track and field team in the school immediately for girls and boys alike. I became interested and tried out for running sprints. It turned out I was considered quite fast for my size and made the team, running the fifty- and one-hundred-yard dash, and also the relay. We competed against other black schools in nearby towns and usually won most of the meets. I won a lot of first place blue ribbons and that added to my popularity around school. Prof, as we called our principal, was liked by everyone and he brought a new sense of pride to all of us.

One day I was sitting on the school steps with one of the guys I hung out with. His name was Howard Russell Campbell but, he had the nickname of Hots. Hots was a mixed kid, half white and black, fat, with feet so flat he had trouble walking. As we sat there talking, he asked me how was it that I could run so fast and could I help him to run fast too. For some unknown reason, I told him the reason I could run so fast was I drink milk with two teaspoons of talcum powder stirred into it. If he did the same thing, he would be able to run fast too. Several days later, his mother told my mother what I had told her son to do and it made him very sick . When I got home from school, Mom met me at the door with two switches from the apple tree and tore into me but good for what seemed like a very long time. My butt was so sore, I couldn't sit down comfortably for a day or so. I was grounded and made to apologize to him and his mother. To make matters worse, she told Prof what I had done and he suspended me from participating in three meets. That hurt more than the whipping.

Hots was a likeable guy, one of the boys. He had quite a sense of humor that was entertaining to us kids and adults alike. He always had an idea or plan to do something that was fun and that made him popular with us. I remember one summer four or five us went to visit another buddy who lived a few miles out of town. We walked and hitch-hiked there and later that day we started walking and trying to hitch a ride back to town. Hots was lagging so far behind us he started complaining because we would not wait for him. We laughed and kept right on walking. A little while later, we saw a pick-up truck coming towards us and as it approached, we stuck out our thumbs for a ride. The white man driving never glanced in our direction and drove past us. After he had passed, we saw Hots sitting in the back, falling out laughing at us with his middle finger stuck out. The driver must have thought Hots was white and stopped for him. We walked all the way back to town.

One summer I asked my Mother if I could go to Carrollton and visit with my father. She seemed surprised that I would want to visit him since he had no time for me when we lived together. Still, I wanted to go see my father for some reason. Mom asked Aunt Boo about it, who in turn contacted Aunt Lin, and in a very short time I was in the passenger seat of an old, rusty pick-up truck driven by a friend of Uncle Louis's, on my way to Carrollton.

When I was dropped off at the house, Aunt Lin met me at the front door, kissed me and took me into the house. She told me my father was asleep and she would awaken him. After shaking him repeatedly, she finally got him awake and told him I was there. I noticed he was drunk and had pissed his pants. The room smelled of urine, tobacco and stale whiskey. He raised up on one elbow, looked at me while rubbing his bloodshot eyes then, managed to say, "Hello there, Robert Leon!" before he fell back on the bed sound asleep.

Unfortunately, the only memories I have of my father are not pleasant ones. During that week's visit, I followed my father into bars where we had to enter the back door because the establishments were white owned. His purpose for being there was to beg for a drink. The owners and bartenders knew my dad because he frequented them regularly to sweep up or some other menial task to get a drink. One bar we entered, the bartender noticed us and greeted him with, "Hello there, Cat White (evidently his nickname), whose that you got with you Little Cat White?" My dad answered, "Yessir, this here is my boy who is visiting me for the week. I was just wondering if you could spare me a little drink for doing some sweeping or trash emptying for you?" He replied, "Naw Cat, I don't need nothing done today, so git on outta here now!" My dad pleadingly asked again, "Well Sir, can't you give me one little shot and I'll come back later when you need some work done?" "Damnit Cat, git the hell on outta here right now and take Little Cat with you!" My father took me by the hand and shuffled out the door. We made several other stops in bars with the same degrading results. I just remember feeling so ashamed of my father.

My father was a fairly intelligent man who possessed an elementary school education. He was well-spoken and likeable, but had fallen victim to alcohol. The depression and segregation had completely defeated him, as it had so many other black men during those years. Unable to provide for their families, they felt defeated and found solace in the bottle. Many deserted their families voluntarily, or were put out by wives who could not tolerate their behavior any longer. They were mostly uneducated with no marketable skills. Manual labor was all they could do, yet couldn't find work doing that. Women were the breadwinners, as they could find work in white homes as cooks and maids. As such, they paid the bills and provided for the general welfare of the family. Food, clothing and anything else that was being discarded by white families, was brought home.

A short time later, Mom received word that my Dad had went to sleep drunk, started coughing, causing a blood vessel to burst in his neck and bled to death. He was thirty-nine years old. I was nine. I don't remember any of us attending his funeral services.

Mom always did the best she could for us, at times working two jobs. She got a job at a black-owned mortuary, styling the hair of female corpses. It was a part-time job, but she made as much, if not more, than she did working as a maid. However, there were some unpleasant consequences she had to endure while working there. She became involved with a mortician, named William Napier. They began dating regularly and Mom seemed happy for the first time in a long time. The money she was making improved our life and her relationship was going good, until he became very jealous and controlling of her. We would hear him cursing and fussing at Mom very loudly, so much so that we all were fearful of him. The arguments became more frequent and more threatening. Now we became concerned about Mom's safety.

One evening he brought her home and the arguing and cursing started. Suddenly he grabbed Mom by the hair and started punching her in the face. Maxine jumped up and ran over to him, crying, "Stop hitting my Mother!" He pushed her back. At that time, I ran over and jumped on his back, wrapping my legs around his waist while pulling his head back with one hand and punching him with the other. By this time, Maxine came back hitting him. My Mother, Maxine and I were all over him until he was forced to leave.

Maxine was tall for her age, big-boned and would fight when she was forced into it. At school she was always being teased and called "Checker Board Head" because her hair was short and Mom parted it off in little square patches then braided it. When it was done, it resembled a checker board. One boy in her class, named Doug Brooks, was considered to be the school bully. He taunted Maxine daily causing her to leave school crying everyday. One day we were walking down the school steps heading home and Doug started in on Maxine. She had had enough, and with tears streaming down her cheeks, turned around, hit Doug in the face with her books she had strapped together, and started punching him all the way down the school steps. He ran off holding his head and that ended his and everyone else's teasing of Maxine. Since I was so small, I wanted it known that Maxine was my sister, in case someone wanted to start something with me. Several times she did come to my defense, thank goodness.

We saw evidence from Moms' bruises that the assaults continued. The most serious incident occurred one summer evening. We were at home alone when a police car pulled up in front of our house. The officer came to the door and asked, "Is this where Benita White lives?" We answered yes and he said, "Well, one of you had better come with me to the station, your Mother is there!" I said I would go. Scared, I got into the squad car with him. Not knowing what to say or ask, I just sat there not saying a word until we reached the station. He led me into the squad room where I saw my Mother sitting in a chair crying and holding a bloody piece of gauze to the right side of her head. I began to cry too as I ask her what had happened. When she removed the blood-soaked gauze to replace it, I saw a big open hole in the side of her temple. Between sobs, she told me William Napier had hit her with a car crank and the police found her bleeding in the street.

Just then a nurse showed up and told me to go back to the front of the station, they were going to stitch up my mothers' wound. An officer on the desk gave me a soda and told me if the wound to Mom had been one inch higher, it would have killed her. She was very lucky. He also said they were looking for William Napier to arrest him and charge him with attempted murder. They never found him, but I'm sure if they would have looked hard enough they could have found him since he worked at the only black mortuary in this small town. Black on black crime was never pursued very vigorously in those days. Yet, I swore that when I became grown, I was going to find him and kill him. After becoming a young man I asked Mom if she or anyone knew of his whereabouts. She said a member of his family told her he had died. I asked her if she could find out where he was buried, I wanted to visit his grave. I didn't tell her why but, I was going to visit his grave and piss on it. I never did find out where he was buried. I was very angry then and still am today.

After that tragic incident, Mom left the mortuary and started working in a laundry, ironing clothes. She found customers who requested she iron for them personally at home, so we were doing a lot better financially. We moved into a slightly bigger house and I was now sleeping on a roll-away bed and not on the floor. We had a grape vine full of grapes in the back yard, a mulberry tree on the side and a limb or two of our neighbors' apple tree spilled over into our yard just loaded with big red apples. No need for apples with rotten spots on them any more.

This was also the first time I remember having a really big Christmas tree, fully decorated and Christmas morning, presents covered the bottom of the tree. I got a nice, big red wagon, a Red Ryder B-B Gun and a sled. I was so very happy, I actually cried. Only two Christmases stand out to me, this one being the best and the worst one was when we lived with Aunt Boo. Uncle Louis went somewhere and cut down a Christmas tree, brought it home and we began decorating it with popcorn we strung and wrapped around the tree from top to bottom. Mom and my sisters cut red and multi-colored pieces of material into small bows, tied with string and wrapped them around the tree. We drew Santa Clauses, angels and stars for the tree too. When we finished, the tree looked really pretty. Filled with Christmas spirit and singing Christmas carols, we were looking forward to Christmas morning and finding the presents we put on our lists under the tree.

We woke up early and ran to the tree, only to find one little present under it. It was about the size of a pie-pan, wrapped very nicely in Christmas paper with a tag on it which read, "To Maxine, Robert, Mildred and Marie, from Santa Claus." Heartbroken, we opened it to find a little red tin train that you wind up, making it go around the little track. My sisters cried and cried and I believe I joined in too, all wondering why Santa didn't like us, we had been good kids and minded our mother. Mom left the room and went outside, I'm sure to be alone and cry.

One summer day several friends and I had climbed up a big tree in our backyard. Climbing trees was a favorite past-time of ours.

We would sit on limbs of trees for hours playing and carving our initials on the limbs. As we sat there, my buddy Hots noticed our grapevine was loaded with big, purple grapes and mentioned that we should make some wine with the grapes. He said he knew how because he watched his older brother making it. Well, it sounded pretty exciting to us so we agreed to do it. Hots said he could get the big, ceramic crock jar to make it in and all the other ingredients needed.

The next day we met in the yard and began picking the grapes and putting them into the jar. We added water and sugar. He told us the jar must be covered and kept in a dark place at all times. So we covered it with a burlap bag and tied a string around it tightly, then stored it under the house, another favorite hangout of ours; where we shot marbles and played mumblety-peg for hours. Hots said it had to sit for weeks to ferment and he would check it periodically.

Weeks went by and my boot-legging buddies and I would take a peek at it at least once a week. We noticed the bubbling and gurgling in the liquid and the aroma was beginning to smell like wine. One day, after what seemed like forever, Hots showed up with a tin cup and summoned the "Under The House Bootleggers" together for an official taste test. We all gathered around the jar, eagerly waiting to test it. Hots dipped the tin cup in, gingerly brushing aside the crushed purple grape skins floating on top of the liquid and submerged the cup into the liquid, retrieving only a small of amount of the wine. He brought the cup to his lips and slowly sipped it. His facial expression did not change as he swallowed it, then told us it was not yet ready, it was too sweet. Maybe a few more weeks and it would be just right. Well of course we trusted his judgment, but we wanted our turn at tasting it too. He passed the cup around and we sampled our first taste of what would soon be real wine.

It was about three weeks later when the final testing took place. We assembled under the house, each armed with his own cup, happily awaiting for them to be filled. Hots made his test and smiled broadly as he swallowed the wine. "Its just right, let's have some!" We skimmed the residue away and immersed our cups into this beautifully colored nectar we had made. The taste was definitely different from before, causing a cough and a bit of a frown on our faces as it went down. But we were undaunted; we sat there in the dirt under the house, and finished our first cupful, then another.

Shortly thereafter, everything anyone said or done was becoming funnier by the minute, causing us to fall out rolling and laughing in the dirt. At some point, we staggered out from under the house and fell out drunk in my front yard where my mother found us when she came home. My sisters said they tried to awaken us but couldn't. They told her that we were yelling loud and using bad language. Maxine mentioned that I had straddled an old abandoned well, with my feet dangling into the well and had threatened to jump in. She said she grabbed me by the shoulders pulled me away from it. The other parents came over and took their drunks home and needless to say, our precious wine was poured out.

I woke up some hours later and noticed it was dark outside. My sisters were playing and my mother was busy in the kitchen. Everything seemed normal. She calmly asked me if I would like something to eat. My stomach felt really messed up and I said no I wasn't hungry. But I noticed she was exceptionally calm and not talkative at all. I know her demeanor all too well, and when she takes on this one, it is definitely the calm before the storm. I knew I had it coming, Big Time! So, as was normal for me, I started sweating profusely and itching in my armpits. I was scared to death just thinking about the beating I was going to get. I always tried to negotiate with my mother when I had done something I knew I would get a whipping for. I always felt we could discuss the issue and arrive at a different punishment solution than the one she had decided on. Mostly, this was to no avail, and I got a butt beating anyway. This time I knew I had no bargaining power whatsoever. This was Bad!!

The night progressed in a normal manner with everyone busy

reading, listening to the radio and playing. I became involved in my drawing and had completely forgotten my earlier transgression and it seemed Mom had too. She never mentioned a word about it and we all went to bed. The next morning Mom was up in the kitchen when she called for me to get up and get some kindling wood to start a fire so she could fix breakfast. As I got up, wearing a thin pair of BVDs, I noticed her walk in from the kitchen with two long switches from the apple tree. She had twisted them tighter and tied the pointed ends together. As she approached me, she started talking to me very calmly, asking me why I did it. I broke out in sweat again and tried to say something as to why I had made and drank the wine, but she really didn't want a reason, she wanted my bare, bony butt. The more she talked, the louder she became. By the time she reached me, I was dancing up and down on one foot and then the other, begging and pleading when the first blow landed on my butt and legs. I kept saying, "Mama I'm sorry, I won't do it no more!" She answered me by saying, "I know damned well you're not going to do it no more, I'm seeing to that right now!" The whipping seemed to go on forever and woke my sisters who just laid in bed watching, except for Marie. She got out of bed, crying asking Mom not to whip me no more. She always cried when Mom whipped me. Mom told her, "Shut up and get your little butt back in bed or I'll give you some of the same thing!" That did the trick.

Along with the whipping, I was grounded for two weeks. I couldn't leave the yard, no friends could come over and I couldn't listen to my favorite radio shows, such as Batman and Robin, Superman, The Lone Ranger and The Shadow. Maxine was in charge of my detention and I couldn't bribe her. That was the longest two weeks of my life and the worst whipping I ever received.

I was at the age where mischief and adventure were what my buddies and I lived for. Halloween provided an excuse for us to be mischievous. Whereas most kids were out Trick or Treating, we never bothered with that childish game. We were just out for the tricking part of it. We went from house to house, throwing bags of dog feces on front porches and turning over outhouses, especially at the homes of people we did not like.

Another favorite past time of ours was going to the movies, whenever our parents could afford the seven cents it costs for us to attend the local movie theater, if you were under eleven years of age. Of course, the theater was segregated, whites on the ground floor and us blacks were crowded upstairs into the steepest, almost straight up rows of stairs and seats imaginable. We would purchase our tickets at a separate window outside then go around the side of the building, up a flight of iron steps resembling a fire escape, then enter the building where a white man stood to take our tickets. Once the movie started, he would leave. Our refreshments, if we had any, consisted of home made Kool-aid put into Mason Jelly Jars, sometimes store-bought sodas, if we were lucky, and popcorn we popped at home. Segregation is acceptable when it's all you know. We were just glad to be there. We got to see an animated cartoon, a news-reel, previews of coming attractions, two full length movies and a continuing serial, such as Zorro, The Green Hornet or the Lone Ranger.

No matter how much we enjoyed the movies, after a while, we became restless and mischievous during intermissions and boring parts of a movie. We would spot white kids sitting downstairs and shoot wadded up spitballs through rolled-up paper blowguns at them and dump popcorn kernels over the railing, once the lights were turned off and the movies continued. They suspected we were doing it on purpose and reported it to the manager, who threatened to throw us out, but our excuse was the seats were located so close and steps were so steep, it was nearly impossible to get into your seat without having something spill or fall on the floor or over the iron railings accidentally. We were very sorry for it happening. Fortunately, no one, to my knowledge, was ever thrown out.

Most of the kids in the neighborhood had very few or no store-bought toys so, we used our imaginations to invent games and create our own toys. One such toy that was popular with us was an automobile tire we would roll along the street while running beside them and using our hands to make them turn the direction we wanted. We all had our favorite tire we used in our races.

Rainy days were a favorite time too. We'd fashion sailboats from popsicle sticks, masts made from paper and fastened them to the mast with a little stick or toothpick. We'd find streams of water trickling down the streets or gutters and have boat races. Some of us kept our little boats year after year.

I had another school buddy, Jimmy Henderson, nicknamed Jappy (he was not Japanese), who lived on a big farm seven to ten miles outside of Marshall. I was intrigued listening to Jappy talk about the daily chores he had to complete before getting ready for school every day. Before daybreak he'd head into the pastures on horseback, round up the cows, herd them into the barn and milk them. Next he would feed the chickens, gather the eggs they had laid, and feed (slop) the hogs before returning to the house for a big breakfast. This sounded like a very exciting life to me, especially riding a horse everyday. My imagination went directly to being a cowboy riding the prairie as I had seen in so many cowboy movies. I asked him if I could come to his farm for a visit and maybe help him with his chores. He thought it may be fun and would ask his parents if it was okay. Excitedly, I ran home and asked my mother if she would allow me to go to the farm for a weekend. I explained to her I would have the opportunity to learn how to milk cows, ride horses, plow and do all the other work farmers do. After days of begging and pleading, she agreed to let me go, if it was okay with the Hendersons. Jappys' father said it would be alright too but, he'd rather I came and spent a couple of weeks during the summer because there would be more work to be done and during that time he could use a little extra help. I was a little disappointed that I couldn't go right away and because summer was a long way off. Still, I was happy about being able to spend two whole weeks working and playing cowboy.

Finally, June came around, school was out and the most exciting summer ever, was about to begin for me. My imagination was out of control, way over the top! I envisioned Jappy and I on horseback, tearing across the many hills at breakneck speed, chasing imaginary bands of Indians off our land, just as I had seen in the movies.

School was out on Friday and the following Monday morning, Mr. Henderson and Jappy arrived at my house mid-morning, in a wooden wagon, pulled by two horses (horse-drawn carts and wagons were commonly seen on the streets of Marshall, alongside automobiles during that time). When I saw them approaching, I said a quick goodbye to my sisters (Mom was at work) and tore out of the door running with my little bag of belongings in my hand. My sisters were probably just as glad to see me go as I was to go. I wouldn't be around to bug them for awhile.

I bounded onto the back of the wagon, saying hello to Jappy and Mr. Henderson at the same time. Mr. Henderson was a tall, thin, and slightly stooped man of a very few words. He made conversation only when it was absolutely necessary. Regardless of his quiet nature, he was a very tolerant and even-tempered man, slow to get riled up. He greeted me with, "Mornin', Suh!" which was his usual greeting to men or boys. This morning he had been to the grocery store to buy their monthly supply of groceries. It usually consisted of staples such as flour, sugar, coffee, salt and pepper, etc., that they bought in large quantities to last for a while. Milk, butter and cheese were home-made, bread was baked and all the meats and vegetables were farm-grown. On the way out to the farm, I found out there was one weakness he indulged in when he came in for his monthly grocery run and that was a loaf of white bread and bologna. Mr. Henderson opened up the bologna, took several slices and put them between two slices of bread and passed the loaf of bread and bologna back to Jappy, without saying a word. We quickly made ourselves sandwiches too and the three of us sat chomping happily on our bologna sandwiches as the horses clip-clopped down the old dirt roads, to the outskirts of town where farm land begins.

We arrived at this older, but sturdy, two-storied white house that could have used a fresh coat of paint or two and were greeted by two barking dogs that followed us down the driveway, around to the back of the house, to the back door where we unloaded the groceries. Jappy was told to take the team of horses to the barn, unharness and care for them. As we climbed upon the wagon seat, Jappy asked me if I would like to take the reins driving the horses to the barn. I jumped at the chance and asked what do I do. He gave me the reins and told me to hold them up then bring them down sharply across the horses' rear ends while saying, "Giddy-yup!" I did, and they started moving straight to the barn without being guided and came to a complete stop in front of the barn door. These horses had performed this routine so many times they had it memorized. Besides, they were looking forward to be freed from their harnesses, rubbed down and fed. Although they had come to a complete stop on their own, I still yelled out, "Whoaaa!" I just wanted to hear myself say it in a powerfully commanding voice. I was already getting pumped up.

I watched as he began unfastening the harnesses and slid them off their backs. I thought, he sure is one smart guy to know all that. All the chains, buckles, hooks and straps made it look very complicated. Afterwards, he picked up two brushes, handing one to me and started showing me how to brush the horses down. As I began my brushing, I suddenly realized how big and gentle these animals were. Otherwise, they could trample us very easily. With this in mind I moved rather cautiously as I went around and under this big animal.

Jappy said we had the rest of the day free and would I like to go swimming and I told him yes. He then asked me if I knew how to swim and I replied, "Uhh, yeah, I think so!' (I had never been swimming in my life but did not want to admit it). "Good, c'mon then, we're going to the swimming hole!" We headed out across a big open field that was surrounded by tall, green cornstalks. Going out further, there was a much larger field covered with wheat, glowing in the sunlight as far as you could see.

We ran until we came upon a small area where there was a fairly good sized muddy pond. Jappy told me it was where the cows came to drink once in awhile, but mostly he and his brother came here to "skinny-dip" on hot days. I had no idea what skinny-dipping was until he explained it to me. As soon as we came close enough, Jappy began running towards the water, taking his clothes off as he went. By the time he reached the edge of the pond, he was stark naked, and jumped right into the water. He disappeared under the muddy water then reappeared further out in the pond, yelling for me to come on in. I stood there kinda frozen and fully-clothed at the edge of the pond, scared to death. The thought crossed my mind, I don't have a clue about how to swim, and now my lie about saying I knew how was going to catch up with me as Jappy watches me drown in this pond. Somehow he talked me into getting undressed. Now he beckoned for me to just jump in and I did. Luckily, where I entered, the water was not very deep; it only came up to my shoulders. I stood there thinking how weird it was to have all that mud oozing between my toes. Jappy began swimming and asked me to follow him across the pond. Not knowing how to swim, I imitated him by walking on the bottom, making swimming strokes with my arms as if I were actually swimming. I thought, "This is working out really cool, he'll never know I cannot swim." As fate would have it, I kept swim-walking following him and came upon a low spot on the bottom and dropped down into water over my head. I panicked and started flailing my arms all about while swallowing mouths-full of muddy water, my eyes were burning and I could not see. I became hysterical and started yelling for Jappy. He came to my aid immediately and pushed me a few feet forward where my feet touched solid ground again. So my lie about being able to swim was found out, but Jappy promised to teach me how to swim before I left the farm.

The next morning before daybreak, Mr. Henderson awakened Jappy and me. Jappy told me we were going to the barn to bridle up a horse, ride out into the pastures and round up the cows for milking. The fact that we were going to be riding a horse caused me to become very wide awake. My imagination kicked in again, envisioning a cowboy riding the range in the moonlight while singing a lonesome cowboy song. My playing cowboy with a broomstick between my legs is a far cry from what was happening now. This is the real thing! I can't find words to tell you how happy this made me.

We went out to the barn and Jappy pulled a bridle down from a hook on the wall and proceeded to where the horses were stabled. He chose a horse, calling it by name and led it out of its stall, then put the bridle on him. He put one of his feet on the siding of a fence and sprung himself upon the horse's back and told me to do the same thing. I did and sat there straddled the horse. After climbing on, I was surprised to find out how high we were off the ground and how wide the horse's back was. My legs were stretched farther apart than they had ever been.

Jappy told me to hold onto his waist as we headed out of the barn and across the barnyard. The horse was walking at a slow pace until Jappy hit him across the back with the leather bridle straps several times yelling out, "Giddyup, c'mon giddy up!" Immediately the horse broke out into a trot across the barnyard. Jappy hit him again harder and yelled out louder than before causing the horse to spring forward into a spirited gallop. It caught me off guard and I was thrown back a bit from Jappy's back, but held on to his waist and pulled myself back in close to him again, bouncing up and down and being jostled from side to side. I noticed chickens starting to cackle as they fluttered their wings, scurrying out of our way as we rode off into the pasture area to round up cows just before daybreak.

We reached the grazing area just as the sun was beginning to lighten the sky with long, hazy yellow and orange streams of sunlight and

Jappy pointed out the black silhouettes of several cows grazing on the horizon. "Yeaahhh, lets go get 'em boy!" Jappy yelled out, as he dug his heels into the horse's side. He broke out in a full gallop heading straight for the cows and almost losing me again, as I slid back onto the horse's rump. We reached them, coming up from behind, causing them to turn into the direction we had just come from. It suddenly dawned on me that this horse was used to this routine as well as the cows and both knew full well what to expect; it happened everyday. It was only exciting to me.

Upon reaching the barn, the cows were herded into stalls for milking. Jappy reached up and took a large pail or bucket from a hook on the wall while grabbing a small wooden stool nearby and told me follow him to the first stall where we would begin milking the cows. To say I was resistant and more than a little skeptical about milking this big beast, is putting it mildly. He noticed my fear and assured me there was nothing to be afraid of; it was really very easy. He told me to watch him first then, do the same thing. Jappy sat on the stool, took both hands and grabbed the cow's teats, pushing them upwards into the udder first; he said this helps start the milk flowing. Next he buried his head between the hollow of the cows stomach and leg and began alternate pulls on the cow's teats and the sound of the milk streams started pinging out loud as the hit the bottom of the bucket. "See how easy it is? Give it a try!"

He stood up, and I slowly sat down on the stool. Reluctantly, I reached out and grabbed one of the teats. It was very warm but the skin was somewhat rough. I squeezed it several times but no milk came out so Jappy had to give me further instructions. After about ten minutes or so, I had it and was milking the cow. Jappy had left me with this cow and started on another of his own. After awhile, Jappy said I should try fresh milk straight from the udder. I said no thanks. He told me to watch as he put his head under the cow's teat with his mouth wide open and sprayed milk directly into his mouth. After some persuading, he talked me into trying it. Naturally, the milk was quite warm, but otherwise it tasted the same, maybe a bit better because it had cream mixed in with it. Once all milk has been taken from cows, the cream rises to the top and is skimmed off for other uses. Often to make butter.

The days on the farm were going by so fast and I was learning so much; how to harness horses to a wagon, put saddles and bridles on them and ride them, milk cows, detassle corn, plow and learn to swim. I felt like a full-fledged farmer and a cowboy. Before the two weeks were up, I was asking if I could stay longer or be able to return next summer. Everything about that life appealed to me. They worked hard and ate good and plenty. Mrs. Henderson would get up early and build a fire in the kitchen stove and prepare one of the biggest breakfasts you've ever seen. There would be eggs, fried potatoes, home-made biscuits, gravy, bacon, ham or sausage and sometimes fried chicken, washed down with fresh milk or coffee you could smell all the way out to the pastures. Lunch, which is called dinner in the mid-west, was equally as big. The women would prepare the food and serve it outside, when the weather was good, on a long, wooden table. The men were summoned from the fields by the clanging of a big iron triangle that hung from the side of the smoke house where meats were stored and smoked. Big pitchers of cold lemonade or ice tea were served along with ham, beef or chicken, mashed potatoes, fresh green beans or some other garden-grown vegetable, macaroni and cheese, green salads, all topped off with home-made ice cream, apple pie or chocolate cake. Then came supper and the whole menu was served over again. There were no small meals on the farm. I had never seen so much food. I often wished my father had been a farmer instead of the town drunk.

The year was 1940. I was going to be eleven years old that December. At that time, my world had become filled with superheroes. Batman and Robin, Captain America, Superman and my favorite, Captain Marvel! I became very good at drawing each of them and spent most of my time drawing. I drew all the characters in the comic section of the paper and anything else I could find. I had a friend who could draw pretty well also and he and I developed our own hero characters. We made our own comic strip and had our characters dueling each other. He would draw on it for a week and give it to me to draw my character defending himself.

Drawing cartoons consumed me during that year and all of the next up to December 7, 1941, when we heard about Pearl Harbor being bombed. The newspapers and the radios were filled with nothing but news of the bombing. All of my radio serial programs were either cancelled or on at different times. I was completely confused. I had no understanding of war, I just knew this sounded really bad. Talk of men being drafted and volunteering to serve in the armed services. Patriotic songs such as, The Army Air Force Song; "Off we go, into the wild blue yonder, riding high into the sky!" The Marines Marching Hymn, "From the Halls of Montezuma to the Shores of Tripoli!" And the Navy's, "Anchors Aweigh My Boys!" were being played constantly. I'm sure this was to get the young men all worked up and ready to go fight and defend the country. Well, it sure had to work for them because it got me marching and saluting with a sense of patriotism and a strong desire to do my part. Over the months after we had started fighting, Hollywood began making movies about the war, depicting the good guys and the bad guys. Of course we were always the good guys and were better looking too. I saw in the movies where the army had used scouts as lookouts in army patrols and on battlefields. I had been reading a few Boy Scout magazines and wanted to become one for some time. I thought this would be a great opportunity for me to become one and be of value to helping in the war. I was really gung-ho about this brilliant idea I had come up with and went straight to my mother with it. It was at this point the wind went right out of my sails. She smiled at me while patting my head and told me no, that's not the kind of scouts they are using, besides, you are much too young.

However, Mom had found a way to assist in the war effort and make more money than she had ever made. She found out about an aircraft manufacturing company in Newport, Rhode Island that was hiring men and women to work building war planes with no experience. She immediately filled out an application which was submitted for approval. Weeks later she received a reply informing her she had the job. Her problem now became what to do about us; who would care for the four of us. Aunt Boo and Uncle Louis were older and their nerves could not handle four young, wild kids.

Mom ended up making arrangements with her sister Alma in Kansas City and Aunt Boo. Aunt Alma would take care of two of us and Aunt Boo, the other two. Aunt Alma was married and had two children of her own but Mom assured her she would send both she and Aunt Boo a monthly allowance for our staying with them. Maxine and Mildred would go to Kansas City and Marie and me would stay in Marshall.

This arrangement had lasted nearly a year when Aunt Boo received a letter from Mom saying the company was laying her off and she would be coming back to Missouri. However, she planned on living in Kansas City because it was a large city and the chances of employment were better there. She would be coming to Marshall for Marie and me soon.

KANSAS CITY, MISSOURI

Marie and I had missed Mom, Maxine and Mildred an awful lot and were happy that we would all be together soon. Marie was always very sensitive and easy to cry. Many nights, during the past months she came to me crying and telling me how much she missed Mom. I always held her and reassured her it would not be much longer before we would all be together in our own home again. When I told her Mama was coming to take us to Kansas City and we all would be living together again, she was very happy.

Before summer was over, we had reunited in Kansas City, living with Aunt Alma. I had completed the sixth grade and would be enrolling in R.T. Coles Junior High and Vocational School as a seventh grader. R.T. Coles was a school where you could continue your academic requirements preparing you for high school or stay there and learn a trade. The school offered a variety of vocational training programs, such as shoe repairing, auto mechanics, barbering, hair styling and cooking. Many parents chose this direction for their children because they believed having a skill was a sure road to a better life. I chose to stick with the academics, graduate and enter high school.

Life in Kansas City was so very different from the small hick town of Marshall. This was a big, metropolitan city. All the streets were paved and had sidewalks, there were small green lawns in front of homes; big three and four storied brick buildings where many people lived. They were called apartment buildings. I had never seen one before. Nearly everyone had a telephone and no party lines.

Every day around mid-morning a man driving a horse and wagon traveled slowly through the neighborhood, clanging a bell and calling out loud and long, "The Huuucksterrr Mannn is Heeereee! Everything I got today is verrry, verry fresh, come and get it!" His wagon was loaded with all kinds of fruits and vegetables. People, mostly women, would stick their heads out yelling, "Hold it right there, Huckster Man!" Soon he would be surrounded by people buying all kinds of fruits and vegetables from him. This became a morning ritual for me. I would get up early when Mom was leaving for work (She had found a job at Union Station working at a soda fountain), sit on the porch and wait for the Huckster Man.

One day I decided to walk down the street, around the corner and over to the next street where I saw my first street car. It looked like a railroad car but had no engine. It stopped, people got on and a conductor closed the doors behind them and off they went, click, click, clicking down the tracks. So now, streetcar watching was added to my morning routine.

One morning, as I was returning from my streetcar watching, my cousin Marvin was sitting on the porch and asked where I had been. I told him I had been watching streetcars coming and going and how much I would like to take a ride on one someday. He said he would ask his mother for some streetcar tokens so we could take a ride. I thought, wow, this would be as exciting as riding a horse. That evening, he asked her and she agreed, only if we would clean up the backyard first. Early the next morning, we were in the backyard pulling weeds, raking up trash and leaves. Aunt Alma came out to inspect it, agreed we had done a good job and handed us two little round, metal coins with a hole in the middle. She said these tokens would allow us to go out to the city zoo and back.

We tore out of the yard running those two blocks as fast as we could to the streetcar stop. I was very excited and did not know what to expect when the streetcar came. After about five minutes or so, I heard the clicking of the wheels on the tracks getting louder and beginning to slow down. Finally, it came to a complete stop in front of us and the other people. Marvin told me to drop the token into the little glass and metal coin box bolted to the floor next to the conductor. I did so and we found a seat. Soon we were pulling away from the stop and picking up speed as we went. The speed continued to increase so much until the car started rocking from side to side on the tracks. I became a bit scared, broke out in sweat and grabbed the back of the seat in front of me. Marvin laughed at me and assured me it was normal and happened all the time.

We reached the end of the line which was where the zoo was located and everyone got off, except us. The conductor came through the car, checking the floor and each seat. He asked if we were returning with him, we nodded and deposited our remaining tokens.

For a brief moment, my mind wandered back to Marshall and my buddies there. I thought, if they could only see me now. I had been a poor country boy who learned to ride horses bare-backed, milk cows, learned to swim in a muddy creek. Now here I am, a city boy, riding on streetcars, eating food cooked on a gas stove, stored in a refrigerator! And last but not least, using an indoor toilet! I realized right then and there, I liked city life much better.

On the block where we lived, there were lots of boys around my age to play with. Aunt Alma's son Marvin was a couple of years younger than me and made sure that I knew all the guys. They asked me where I lived before coming there. I lied and told them I came from Marshall, Texas (somewhere I had heard of a town in Texas named Marshall). I told them there were lots of cowboys there and I rode horses almost everyday. They seemed impressed and hung onto every word I said. The only reasons I can think of for telling that big lie was, I was beginning to recognize that I was much smaller that the other guys my age and I wanted to stand out and be accepted, regardless of my size. Secondly, I had seem cowboy movies that were supposedly, made in Texas and I wanted to be one so badly.

Playing cowboys and Indians in Marshall was a favorite game of ours. My favorite cowboys were Johnny Mack Brown and Hopalong Cassidy. I liked The Lone Ranger and Tonto too, but a friend of mine would never let me be The Lone Ranger. I was always Tonto, and I got tired of that.

Well, my needless lie didn't seem to matter any at all to these guys since they were not into playing cowboy at all. So my interest in cowboys drifted to buying and reading comic books. Super Heroes flying through the air took the place of cowboys riding their horses along dusty trails. Superman, Batman and Robin, Captain Marvel and many others held my attention these days. My preoccupation with superheroes and their supernatural feats were causing my imagination to grow to such unrealistic proportions, I was starting to believe I could perform some of these feats.

Captain Marvel was my favorite. Dressed in his red form fitting tights with yellow boots and cape, he could say the magical word, "Shazam!" and take off flying. I believed I was capable of doing the same thing. So one day, my sisters and I were walking along a street that had an overpass. Underneath the overpass were lots of railroad tracks. As we walked along, I got the wild idea to climb upon the narrow concrete railing and walk across. I got on the railing, stood up and started walking across, ignoring the train tracks below. My sisters began yelling and pleading for me to get down. To calm their fears, I told them not to worry, if I lose my balance and start to fall, all I have to do is shout out, "Shazam!" and I would start flying, landing safely on the ground. Luckily, I made it.

Marvin was instrumental in me becoming acclimated to life in Kansas City. He took me for my first swim in the public swimming pool located in Paseo Park. How different this was from where I learned to swim in that muddy old pond on Jappy's family farm. I could actually swim under water with my eyes open without them burning and dive into the pool from a diving board, not from a tree limb or the side of a bank. We spent most of our summer afternoons at Paseo Park, swimming.

When we were not swimming, we were allowed to go to the movies on Saturday afternoons. There were two or three movie theaters in Kansas City that were for black people only. They were located on 18th Street, a very busy street for night life. This is where all the night clubs and dance halls were and all the well-known musicians of the day performed; Duke Ellington, Count Basie, Charlie Parker, Nat Cole and many, many others.

Many a Saturday afternoon, Marvin and I would walk up 18th Street and stop at Vine Street to listen outside to the music coming from inside the clubs. We'd hear people shouting, singing and dancing. The beat got to us too, and before we knew it, we were dancing on the sidewalk, too. On several occasions, the doorman would good naturedly shoo us away, saying, "You boys are too young to be out here, go on home!" Other times, he would be dancing and snapping his fingers, so carried away by the music, he just let us stay. I never realized this exposure would have a lasting effect on me. I found myself going down there by myself just to listen every chance I got and eventually learning the words to some of the songs. Seems as though my mother's show business genes were beginning to sprout in me.

My sister Maxine was a big Frank Sinatra fan and introduced me to his music during the war. I had learned a lot of his early hits when she and I would sit on the front porch in the evening singing along with him. These were the early war years, and her boyfriend at the time was overseas with the army, so mostly all the songs were slow, sad ballads that brought tears to her eyes as she sang them. Whereas, the music I was listening to on 18th and Vine was up tempo and made you want to move.

Mom had been home from Rhode Island only a short time before we moved out of Aunt Alma's house and into an apartment of our own two blocks down the street. It was early 1945 and I was entering my third and final year at R.T. Coles. My total focus was on my art. I wanted to continue through high school and college majoring in art. My goal was to become a comic book artist or a cartoonist for Walt Disney.

It was around this time that Maxine wrote her boyfriend, serving somewhere in Europe, a "Dear John" letter (breaking up with him). She had been dating Wilbur Henderson, Jappy's older brother, became pregnant and wanted to move back to Marshall and marry him. She and Mom argued constantly about her actions; about how hard she has had to work raising us and this is how she showed her appreciation. Mom was very hurt but could not convince Maxine to stay. I suppose, somewhere during one of their many arguments, Mom realized she had started her life pretty much the same way and relented.

As a waitress in a busy lunch counter in Union Station, Mom met and served customers coming and going on trains; those who were greeting passengers or seeing them off. Quite often she would serve some people regularly and get to know them fairly well. One such man she became fairly well acquainted with was a regular customer. He ate lunch there each time he came into Union Station from Los Angeles, California, which was a couple of times monthly. After becoming acquainted a bit, their conversations became more personal. He was married but had no children. Mom mentioned being divorced and raising four children, three girls and a boy. She bragged about me, saying she thought I was quite gifted in art and that I wanted to become a professional artist. She proceeded to take a picture that I had drawn from the wall of the soda fountain and showed it to him. He agreed it was very good for a child of fourteen years of age and asked if he could take it to California with him and show his wife. Mom agreed and gave him the drawing.

When she came home, she told me this man was very interested in my art and wanted to take one of my drawings with him to California. She had allowed him to take the drawing, thinking he just may want to help further my art training. I didn't think much of it at the time and soon forgot about it completely.

About two months later, Mom came home with a man, a very short, rotund, copper-colored grey-haired man, wearing thick bifocal glasses. He held his head somewhat elevated, possibly to make him appear taller, but had a warm, friendly smile on his face as he stared at me. "Robert, this is Mr. Venerable, Mr. Venerable, my son Robert," Mom said. Still smiling, he reached out his hand saying, "Very nice to meet you, Robert. Your mother has told me a lot about you!" Looking into his eyes, as he was about my height, I shook his hand and replied, "Nice to meet you, too!"

"Robert, Mr. Venerable is the man I told you about who is interested in your drawings and wants to see some more. Go get some and show him!" I left the room and returned with several of my drawings and handed them to him. He perused each one very slowly, still smiling and after a while, looked up and said, "Robert, I think you have quite a talent here and I would like to help you further your art training in schools that would be very beneficial to you. Your mother and I have talked quite a bit about this, and if you agree, I would like to bring you to Los Angeles, California to live with my wife and me, where you can continue your training. I know this is very sudden for you, so take your time and think it over, talk it over with your mother and if you decide to do it, I will send you a train ticket when school is out this summer and you can start school in California in the fall. In the meantime, I would like to take more of your drawings home with me for my wife to look at."

I was shocked and did not know what to say. I just stared at him and mumbled a, "y-yessir!" This was one hell of a decision for a fourteen year old to make. The thought of leaving my mother and sisters to go 1,500 miles across the country to live with someone I had known for less than one hour, was really scary to me, yet kind of exciting. I had read of Los Angeles, California and Hollywood in the movie magazines my sisters loved to read. I saw the pictures of glamorous movie stars posing under orange trees loaded with big, juicy oranges. People walking down the streets lined with tall swaying palm trees; lying on a sunny beach overlooking the Pacific ocean. Plus, I heard it never snowed in California, the weather was warm and sunny all year long. All this heavily influenced my decision to go.

All this, and the fact that I would be going to a school for art, drawing all day, every day. No more boring, stuffy history classes, the complicated, math classes or any of the other classes I was taking that were totally unrelated to making a living as an artist. Taking all of these things into consideration, a few days later I told my Mom that I thought I wanted to go. She assured me life would be much better for me there.

Mr. Venerable could provide for me very well since he was a wealthy man. I would have my own room. Can you imagine, me with my own room! No more pallets on the floor, no more roll-away beds! Yes, I definitely wanted to go.

There was still one more month of school and I would be graduating from the ninth grade. Time seemed to stand still as I spent everyday preoccupied with my big move to California to study art. Marvin and the rest of my buddies listened to me intently as I talked about what my life would be like when I reached California. Of course, I exaggerated to make it more interesting.

Finally, graduation day arrived and I marched with my class in cap and gown onto the big football field as the band played Pomp and Circumstance. It made me feel really proud and a little sorry that I would be leaving the school where I had spent the last three years, my friends and ultimately, the city, very soon.

Mom had begun to save a little money each week to buy me new socks, underwear and a few pants and shirts. She said she did not want me packing old ragged underwear and socks with holes in them. She was going to throw them away. She said by the time Mr. Venerable sent my ticket in August, I would have all the things I needed.

Again, time seemed to stand still. Summer dragged on. I spent my time with Marvin and the guys on my block swimming, playing ball in the streets and a new found interest, marching. One of the boys who lived across the street from me, Claude Hendricks had joined the R.O.T.C. in high school. He was a member of the elite trick drilling squad. The marching they did was not just routine drilling but very fancy. We became interested in it, mainly because of the war. As a result, Claude had organized a squad of eight or ten of us to form a drilling squad. For hours he trained us, barking out commands as we marched back and forth up and down the brick street. Eventually, we became very good at performing fancy drill routines and attracted the attention of neighbors in the block. Weekend evenings they would sit on their porches and lawns watching and applauding as we paraded up and down the street. The more they showed their approval of us, the more we strutted to the cadence with an accentuated rhythmic step on counts one and three. Claude would sing out rhyming ditties in time with the cadence, such as, "Ain't no use in going home, Jody's got your gal and gone, so sound off!" Then we would count in time with our steps, "One, two, three, four... one, two (pause)... three four!" Marching became my favorite pastime, but I knew I would be leaving for California soon and would have to give it up.

The month of June dragged by and July crawled to an end. Now it was August and I was on pins and needles expecting the letter from Mr. Venerable with my train ticket in it. Every morning I could be found sitting on my porch steps at 2452 Tracy Avenue, drawing from comic books while waiting for the mailman to deliver the letter that would change my life. I had shared with him the importance of the letter I was expecting and morning after morning he would say to me, "Sorry Robert, that letter didn't make it today, maybe tomorrow!" I was beginning to get a little depressed, and starting to think maybe he had forgotten about me or changed his mind. If it didn't happen, how could I ever face my friends after all the bragging I had done.

One Wednesday morning Marvin and Claude asked if I wanted to go swimming with them. I thought why not, so I grabbed my swimming trunks, a towel and headed out to the pool with them. As we were walking home a couple of hours later, I saw the mailman delivering his mail and walking towards us. He spoke and turned to me with a big smile on his face and said, "Oh, by the way Robert, I dropped a letter in your mailbox postmarked, Los Angeles, California. It just may be the one you've been waiting for!" I jumped up and down, thanked him and tore out running towards the house. I hit the top of the three steps, missing the first two, stopping at the mailbox. I pulled all the mail out, nervously sorting through it until I found the one I was looking for. It was addressed to my mother with a return address stamped; C.B. Venerable, 2266 South Harvard Blvd. I said to Marvin and Claude who had now joined me, "This is it, this is really it! I'm going to California!"

I held the letter up to the sun to see a short handwritten letter and what appeared to be a check or money order. Normally, I wouldn't think of opening mail addressed to my mother, but I knew this letter was all about me, so I proceeded to open it. Ignoring the letter, I focused on the other slip of paper that was a check made out to Mom for three hundred dollars.

Mom came home around six o'clock that evening, read the letter then looked at me smiling, with tears in her eyes and said, "Mr. Venerable has sent the money for your train ticket and you are to catch the Super Chief Monday morning. So we've got five days left to get you packed up and ready to go to California!"

Again, my imagination kicked in as I thought of sunny days all year long, no more snow, eating big, juicy oranges off of trees, running freely on sandy beaches, swimming in the Pacific Ocean and looking at gorgeous movie stars everyday. All this and studying to become a cartoonist working for Walt Disney drawing the Disney characters. This was not too far-fetched because after all, Walt Disney was from Kansas City, too.

The only down side to all this was, I knew no one there. I'm leaving all my buddies behind. I'm leaving all my family. Completely alone in a strange city, living in a house with people I don't know. How will they treat me? Will they like me? Then there is the problem of enrolling into a new school. Will they think I am weird? Will I dress like they do? Will they know I am from out of town? Now I'm thinking of all the new things I will have to adapt to and it scares me a little. For a brief moment, I had the thought of backing out, telling Mom to send the money back saying I've changed my mind. But then, I can't do that, Mom has sacrificed and bought me all these clothes for the trip. I think, "What have I got myself into?" All these doubts and fears cause me to break out in a light sweat. I'm downright scared! Now I realize, what a big step this is for a fourteen-year-old to take. I went to bed with these worries swimming around in my head for hours before falling off to sleep.

The next four days passed rather uneventfully, but I filled them with talking about the wonders of California to my sisters and friends who listened intently. This false bravado helped me deal with the many insecurities I had regarding the trip and my new life.

Monday morning, Mom woke me up at 5:30 A.M. and had my bowl of Wheaties, the Breakfast of Champions, ready for me to eat. My suitcase was packed and we were ready to leave around seven o'clock. Everyone began hugging and kissing me goodbye with wishes of good luck, be a good boy and write to your Mother often. I promised I would. My sentimental sister Marie, started her boo-hooing and holding onto me sobbing, "Brother, don't leave us, I am going to miss you so much, please don't go!" Her emotional outbursts didn't help matters any for me, but Mom calmed her down. I assured her I would send her postcards with pictures of trees and oranges growing on trees.

Mom and I left home carrying the one little brown cardboard suitcase with tattered corners, heading for the streetcar that would take us directly to Union Station. We arrived there around seven-forty-five and went to the soda fountain where Mom worked. Once there, she made me a nice tuna sandwich, put it into a brown paper bag along with a couple of chocolate cookies and a bottle of strawberry soda. She told me this was my lunch to take with me on the train.

The train was scheduled to pull out of the station at eight-thirty, so we started walking towards the boarding area. Suddenly a Pullman Porter, dressed in a white coat, black pants and black cap, walked up beside us and spoke to my mother, "Good morning, Benita! Is this the big day your son is going to California?" She knew him by name and answered, "Hi there, Henry! Yes, this is the big day I was telling you about! Robert, this is Mr. Henry, he is one of my customers and he works on all the trains, going everywhere!" I smiled and mumbled a hello. I could tell right away, by the way he talked and looked at Mom, he was attracted to her. "You know Benita, my run today is to Los Angeles too, the same train that Robert is leaving on. I could kinda look after him a bit, if you'd like!" Mom thought it might be a good idea and thanked him for offering. She turned to me and told me to let Mr. Henry know if anything was wrong or if I needed anything along the trip. I nodded in agreement.

Shortly, we reached the car where I was to board the train. Mom began giving me lots of motherly advice such as; be a good boy, and mind your manners, bathe regularly and change your socks and underwear daily. (I was notorious for wearing socks too long making my feet stink, according to my sisters, and limiting my bathing to my face and hands.) Lastly, don't forget to write. I promised to remember to do everything she asked.

With a big, long hug and kiss (which I wiped off immediately), I stepped aboard the coach, with Mr. Henry carrying my suitcase and telling Mom not to worry, I was in good hands. A white conductor in an all-black uniform and cap with silver buttons on it approached us, speaking to Mr. Henry and inquiring as to who I was. Mr. Henry told him I was the son of a friend of his and he would be watching over me until we reached Los Angeles. The conductor looked at me and spoke in a dry, unfriendly tone, "Howdy Boy! Let me have your ticket!" I fumbled in my shirt pocket for the ticket and handed it to him. He looked at it and stated, Hmmmm, lets see, 28B, that'll be your seat number. You walk to the back of this coach until you come to 28B. You got it?" I replied, "Yessir, I got it!" I turned and walked, with my lunch bag and soda to my seat and sat down. Momentarily, Mr. Henry came back to where I was sitting and told me he had taken care of my suitcase and not to worry about it. He said we were pulling out of the station now and he had some work to do, but would see me later.

As the train slowly began to move, I glanced out the window and saw my mother smiling up at me, waving and wiping tears from her eyes. It made me sad to see my mother looking so sad. My impulse was to get up and get off the train before it started moving too fast and stay there with her. I realized that was not possible as the doors to the train were all closed. Mom started walking alongside the train keeping her eyes on me, as it slowly departed the station. She started walking faster and faster, as the train began to move. The last image I saw of her was a very small one with her arm waving back and forth. The train moving down the tracks started clickety-clacking faster and faster and soon the view of the station and its surroundings disappeared. We were on our way and I was already getting that sinking lonesome feeling in my stomach.

So, here I was leaving Kansas City Missouri with my small tattered suitcase, a tuna sandwich, a now very warm bottle of strawberry soda and fifteen dollars, which I was instructed to use sparingly for food. I was told not to eat the big breakfasts I loved to eat at home because I would run out of money before I reached California. I was so fascinated by the train ride, it took my appetite for a while. After we were fully underway and the speed was constant, the clickety-clack of the tracks had a constant rhythm, which I started singing Chatanooga-Choo-Choo to. It seemed to fit so perfectly. I wished my mother and sisters were here to sing along with me, like we used to do, many nights at home.

By afternoon, hunger pangs hit me and I pulled out my tuna sandwich and began to eat it. I had just started eating when Mr. Henry showed up and handed me a big, red apple, telling me it would go good with my lunch. He also took my bottle of warm strawberry soda with him and returned with it poured into a glass filled with ice cubes. I thanked him and continued to enjoy my lunch.

Mr. Henry kept his word about taking care of me. Throughout the trip he saw that I had plenty to eat. Both of the following mornings, he took me into the dining car for breakfast and I never had to pay one cent. He always told me, "Don't worry about it, it's taken care of!" At night, he made sure I was comfortable and warm. My seat converted into a bed and he added an extra blanket and pillow. I was quite comfortable and the gentle rocking back and forth of the train, lulled me into a deep sleep. I was truly enjoying this trip.

LOS ANGELES, CALIFORNIA

Early the final morning, Mr. Henry approached me to say we were coming into the state of California and I might enjoy looking out the window to see the palm trees.

Naturally, I had never seen a palm tree, only in pictures, and raised my window shade to take a look. There, as far as I could see, were rows of tall palm trees, swaying in the gentle morning breeze. I was really impressed already, knowing there was much more to come that I had never seen. Moving along, the landscape gradually changed with the addition of groves of green trees loaded with, you guessed it, oranges! ORANGES!! On both sides of the train were these groves just loaded with oranges. I was beside myself with excitement now. I ran from one side of the coach to the other trying to see it all. Just what I had hoped to see, but more than what I had imagined. Immediately I thought, if only my mother, sisters and friends could see what I am seeing. Amazingly beautiful!! I wished I had a camera to take pictures of the whole scene, because writing about it would not do it justice. I would not be able to find the words.

I stayed glued to the window until the train slowly pulled into Union Station in downtown Los Angeles. Mr. Henry came to my seat and asked if I had enjoyed my trip and what I thought of California so far. I thanked him for all he had done for me during the trip (minding my manners as I was told to do) and I really liked what I had seen of California, especially seeing oranges growing on trees. I told him I wished I would have had a camera to take some pictures to send home to my mother and friends. He assured me that would not be necessary, since inside the station and all over the city you could buy postcards of the orange groves, the mountains and the ocean.

Mr. Henry had retrieved my little suitcase and told me to follow him into the station. I walked along light beige, tiled corridors with colorful Mexican and/or Spanish murals painted on them from the floor to the ceiling. Everything was painted brightly, no drab colors like in Kansas City.

I was so busy looking in all directions at everything, that I did not see Mr. Venerable coming towards us and calling my name. "Hello Robert, glad you made it alright! Did you enjoy the train ride?" I assured him I did. Mr. Henry introduced himself and informed him he knew my mother and told her he would look out for me during the trip.

Mr. Venerable thanked him for having done so, and I am not certain, but I think I saw Mr. Venerable press some money into his hand as they were in the process of shaking hands.

Mr. Venerable and I walked through this cavernous building, out into what was a gray, overcast Southern California morning, weaving our way through lines of yellow cabs parked at the curb, red caps loading and unloading luggage, people greeting people, mingled with tearful good-byes. We entered a large parking lot, coming to a stop beside a large, shiny, four door gray Hudson car. Mr. Venerable unlocked the doors and said, "Well, here we are, throw your suitcase in the back seat and we can be on our way home!"

Home. Instantly, the word caused me some unexpected discomfort. It dawned on me that I did not know where home was, what it looked like, how to get there, and I would be walking in on a house full of strangers. As a matter of fact, everyone I would be meeting now, would be strangers. No more familiar faces. The thought scared me.

Leaving the Union Station parking lot, we headed west on a wide, palm tree lined street, passing commercial buildings, churches and homes, all painted different pale pastel colors, green, beige, brown and even pink! I had never seen anything like this in Missouri. Lawns, surrounding the homes and buildings were neatly trimmed and green, outlined with colorful flower beds. I thought I would break my neck trying to take it all in. It was all very pretty.

Our drive had lasted roughly thirty to forty minutes before Mr. Venerable turned off Adams Boulevard, onto LaSalle Avenue then up a short, winding hill that opened into Harvard Boulevard. The homes on Harvard were large, two storied, spacious ones that set back from the sprawling, well manicured front lawns. Once atop the hill, he made a right turn into a horse-shoe shaped driveway, stopping at the front door of 2266 South Harvard Boulevard, a two-storied, stuccoed pale pink house.

I didn't say anything because I couldn't. I'm sure the expression on my face said it all. I was so awe-struck at the sight of this big, gorgeous house and to think I would be living in it. The homes of white people in Missouri could not compare to this. I was also thinking how to tell my family and friends about it and would they believe I was exaggerating about it, or straight out lying.

I sat in the car not moving until Mr. Venerable looked at me smiling and said, "This is home, Robert! C'mon, let's get out and meet the rest of the family." Clumsily, I got out, grabbed my suitcase and we started walking towards the large, ornately decorated wooden entrance. Before we reached the door, it opened and out walked a rather stout, light-complexioned lady, dressed in a colorful, casual dress. Her hair was mixed grey and black and styled with a large bun in the back. She approached us with a wide, toothy smile, and outstretched arms to greet her husband. She stepped towards me, bent over hugging my shoulders and said, "Well, hello Robert! Welcome to California; we're so glad to have you. I am Blaine's wife, Beatrice. Blaine (She called Mr. Venerable by his middle name. Later, I learned that friends and associates referred to him as, C.B.) has told us so much about you and your artistic ability. From what I have seen, you have great potential. I am a teacher and taught in the school system for eighteen years until my asthma forced me to retire. I'm sure the California school system will be helpful in furthering your art training."

Stepping aside, she said, "Now, let me introduce you to the rest of the family. They are my sisters." At that time, I noticed two other older ladies standing in the doorway. Both very light-complexioned, one tall and very slender, dressed in a very conservative, high collared dress. Her hair was grey also and worn piled up on her head with a tight knot on top. Mrs. Beatrice introduced her as Gertrude but everyone called her Gertie. She came forward and with a little shy smile, shook my hand while saying, "Nice to meet you, Robert," then shrunk back into the doorway. "Gertie takes care of the household duties for us," Mrs. Beatrice informed me. "Next, this is our great cook, who keeps us all healthy. Robert, this is Lillian!" Lillian, shorter than the others and much heavier but possessed the same complexion and hair style, came up to me with a warm, friendly smile and gave me a big hug. She seemed more sincere than the others and I liked her right away. While hugging me, she said "Welcome to our home, and I'm going to put some meat on those bones of yours!" Everyone laughed, including Mr. Venerable.

"Let's all go inside and I can show Robert to his room so he can settle in before lunch." I followed him through this finely furnished living room with highly polished floors and plush oriental area rugs. On one side of the room, I noticed a piano, painted a rich golden yellow with ornate brown trim around the edges. (Later I found out it was a self-playing piano.) We continued walking into the kitchen and into a room off the side of the kitchen, which they told me would normally be the quarters for a hired maid or cook. Since the sisters were family and did the cooking and cleaning, they had bedrooms upstairs. The room was average size and completely furnished. It had its own bathroom! There was a face bowl, tub and a shower all with hot and cold running water. Located on the bedside table was a little radio. Now I could listen to my radio shows and serials; Jack Armstrong, the All-American Boy, Green Hornet, Lone Ranger and many others. This was more than I could have imagined. I was in seventh heaven and couldn't wait to write Mom about it.

Aside from moments of being homesick, I was adjusting to life with the Venerables pretty good. Lillian was true to her word about feeding me good, healthy food. She started me eating vegetables, such as cauliflower, broccoli, and brussel sprouts, convincing me they were good for me and would help me to grow (yes, I was still small for my age and underweight. I would do anything if it was going to help me grow). As I got better acquainted with Lillian and Gertie, I found out that they had quite a sense of humor and teased me a lot. They were nice.

Mr. Venerable had assigned me chores to do around the house. They were to empty the trash and burn it in the incinerator (every home had one in their backyard in those days), water the front and back lawn and wipe the car off before we went to church on

Sundays.

The church sponsored a Boy Scout troop which I joined. Mr. Venerable bought me a uniform and all the scouting equipment I needed. I really loved being a Boy Scout and all the activity we became involved in. During the summer we went to summer camp for two weeks where we slept in pup tents and learned to make a fire by using flint stones, then cook our food on open flames. We also learned a lot of survival techniques that are beneficial to this day. My tent mate was always a guy named Maurice Roberts with whom I had a lot in common. At night when other guys were sleeping playing around in their tents, he and I were learning to tie all the knots scouts were required to know or practicing boxing the compass (learning the directions of all 360 degrees on a compass). When all these special skills were learned, we received merit badges for each, qualifying us to be promoted to the next level of scouting.

Once, he and I built a race car from orange crates and roller skate wheels to enter into the Soap Box Derby that was held once a year. We completed our car and entered the contest. It was held on Overhill Drive in Los Angeles, a downhill street nearly two miles long. The street was cordoned off, restricting any vehicular traffic during the races. Maurice and I entered our little car with the many others. When our heat came up, with three other cars, we took our places in the car, one seated behind the other.

Maurice was driving and I was pushing us off. When the starter dropped the flag, I started running as fast as I could, pushing the car to pick up speed, then jumped on.

As the grade became steeper, our speed increased, but to no avail. The other cars, better made, were whizzing by us as if we were standing still. We finished the race, but no ribbon. It didn't matter, we got our merit badges just the same. There was no prouder moment than when we went to the annual Scout-O-Rama and stood at attention before scouting council members in uniform with our merit badge sashes draped over one shoulder and hanging down in front, displaying the many badges we earned for special achievements in scouting.

Maurice and I rose to the rank of Star Scout, became Explorer Scouts and Junior Assistant Scoutmasters to new troops just starting up. I stayed with the Boy Scouts until I went into the Navy. Scouting was an integral part of my boyhood for which I am most proud.

Mr. Venerable also bought me a bicycle that I rode from morning till night. One of my favorite stops was at a drug store down the hill on Adams Boulevard that had a soda fountain. I stopped there at least once a week to buy a big chocolate malt and a hamburger. The malts were so big and thick they reminded me of the ones Mom used to make for me when I visited her at the Union Station Snack Bar. As I sat there sipping my malt, I became rather homesick and lonesome for my mother and sisters.

Mr. Venerable's business was operating transient hotels. Rooms were rented by the hour, day or week. They were rented by men who brought women or prostitutes in and made love to them for short periods of time. The maids he had working there were constantly removing soiled bed linens. He owned and operated three of them in the Little Tokyo section of downtown Los Angeles and they stayed busy. He acquired them as a result of all Japanese being rounded up in 1942 and forced to evacuate their homes, close down their businesses and sent to relocation camps located in several states throughout the United States. The government deemed them a threat to the country since we were at war with Japan. Mr. Venerable had been quite friendly with a Japanese man who owned three hotels, and a mutual verbal agreement was reached between the two of them. He agreed to buy the hotels for a small amount of money, operate them until the war was over, then return them for the same price. The deal was sealed with a handshake. Mr. Venerable was running the hotels when I arrived in August of 1945 and had become rather wealthy.

Boy Scout Troop #131 party. Me, sitting in front, next to girl in plaid skirt.

One day Mr. Venerable took me with him to one of his hotels. Along the way he explained a job he wanted me to do for him, for which he would pay me. He wanted me to ride my bicycle to each of the hotels, pick up the cash receipts for the day and take them home. I felt a little nervous about carrying all that money through the streets on a bicycle. He said he thought I would be alright. He made the rounds to all three hotels, introduced me to the managers and explained what I would be doing.

My first day of collecting the money went well. It was given to me in a paper bag, wrapped with rubber bands. Once I collected from all three hotels, I combined the money into one big grocery bag bound with a much heavier rubber band and headed for home. When I arrived, I took the money upstairs to his bedroom where he kept all the money stacked in shoe boxes in his closet. I emptied the bags of money onto a desk, counted each stack and recorded it into a big ledger book. I then placed the money into a shoebox and placed it in the closet with the other boxes of money. I felt somewhat important and pleased that he put that much trust in me.

I was given an allowance of five dollars a week which I spent on hamburgers and sodas, comic books and drawing pads, but I lucked into another money-making situation. While riding my bike down Harvard Boulevard, a heavyset black lady yelled at me, "Hey Boy, come here a minute!" I looked over and saw her standing beside a fancy white 4-doored Jaguar. I turned my bike around and rode over to where she was parked. She asked me if I would like to make some money unloading her groceries and carrying them into her house. I said, "Yes Ma'am!" She opened the trunk and showed me the bags of groceries. I removed the groceries and carried them into her house through the rear door, placing them on a large table in the kitchen. She thanked me and handed me a crisp ten dollar bill and told me to look for her car parked out front on Saturdays and quite likely she would have groceries to be unloaded. I thanked her and told her I would. With a big smile, I rode home and told Mr. Venerable about my good fortune. He smiled and asked me if I knew who the lady was. I told him I had no idea who she was but, I described her and pointed to the house where she lived. Then he told me she was Hattie McDaniels, the movie star who had won an Oscar for her role in the movie, "Gone With the Wind." I was speechless and couldn't wait to write home and tell my mother and sisters about it. Mr. Venerable then told me Rochester lived near by and an older black actress named Louise Beavers had a home on the next street over. Later I found out this section of Los Angeles was an exclusive upscale neighborhood called Sugar Hill where lots of show business people lived.

Another big hurdle to jump was staring me in the face. It was time to register for school. A new school, new kids, and me, the new kid in town. We had decided I would go to Manual Arts High School. I stupidly thought because the word arts was a part of the name, it was a school dedicated to training in the arts. Mr. Venerable drove me to the school and I got the biggest shock of my life! There were all these kids laughing talking and milling about on the campus, White, Asian, Mexican, Black! I thought, what is this!! I asked Mr. Venerable, Are all these different kinds of kids going to this school? He answered me saying, "Why yes, Robert, I thought you knew the schools in California are integrated." I froze in my tracks, afraid to move. My heart was beating so hard, I could hear it above the noise. I broke out in sweat and thought I was going to pass out. I had never talked to any kids white or Mexican and I had never, ever seen an Asian person, except in movies. If there were any in Kansas City, I never saw them.

Oh boy, crisis time. What do I do? Mr. Venerable took my sweaty hand and said, "C'mon, let's go. You can handle it." We walked up to the registrar's office and attempted to register, but found I could not because I did not live in that school district. Students must attend the school that's in the district where they live. I was told the school district I live in is Polytechnic High School.

I enrolled in Poly High and I must admit, the adjustment to an integrated school was much less painful or traumatic than I imagined. Kids of all ethnic backgrounds and cultures were enduring the same doubts and fears I suffered, not because of the racial issue, but because it was their first year in high school. The upper classmen, juniors and seniors gave us flack constantly. We were called "Scrubs," the lowest of the low, and they did not care what color you were, where you came from or what your name was. Your name was Scrub and that's how you would be identified and addressed by them.

Life with the Venerables was going okay, but I was beginning to get pretty lonesome for my family. Mr. Venerable knew it and without my knowledge, had been in touch with my mother. He had arranged for my mother and two sisters to move to California. Maxine was now married, with newly-born baby girl, and would not be coming.

During the summer after my first year in California, my mother and sisters arrived and moved into a rooming house Mr. Venerable had bought. He had given my mother a job as a maid in one of his hotels. I was very happy and wanted to move in with them. Mr. Venerable understood and agreed to let me move. Besides, the war was over, and the Japanese were returning to their respective homes and businesses. As a result, Mr. Venerable began turning the hotels over to the original owner as per the agreement. For the last three or four years, he made a fortune, and was now contemplating opening new businesses.

The first two years went by rather uneventfully and I settled into my school routine. I had made friends with guys and girls of other ethnic groups and was offered the job of cartoonist on the school paper, which I accepted immediately. This distinction afforded me quite a bit of popularity. I wanted to gain my popularity playing sports, football or track, but I was too small to make either team. However, in my junior year, I became water boy for the varsity football team. It was not the most glamorous job, handing out towels to the sweaty, bloody players and rushing in with a water bucket, but I was on the field.

I took pride in being known as one of the most popular artists in school. As such, I was chosen to design the cover of our class yearbook. With my newly acquired popularity as an artist, I became outgoing and quick-witted. I drew funny cartoons to show the guys on campus during the lunch hour. It was also during this time that a certain group of guys would start "Wolfing" sessions. Wolfing was the name given to the practice of making fun of and degrading another guy's mother and other members of his family, but mostly it was about their mother. Certain guys would ask me to draw ugly, fat, out-of-shape, bare-footed women, wearing ragged clothes. They would bring them to the "Wolfing Circle" to show the other guys and pick one guy out, telling him this was his "Mama." It always drew a big laugh from the others, but they knew I was the one who had drawn it. Consequently, they would get on my case pretty badly; chasing me around the campus for awhile. Somehow, before long, I was put into the middle of this and they began talking about "My Mama" too. They got their laughs but they couldn't outdo me, because I would talk about their mothers then produce an ugly picture I had drawn and get the biggest laugh of all. Because of this, I was dubbed "The King of Wolfing."

Still, this offbeat title and popularity did not make me popular with the girls. I did not have a girlfriend nor could I get a date. My size was a big drawback for me. Girls my size were dating the big jocks. One day during the lunch hour I asked a girl, who was much taller than me, but was always very friendly towards me, if she would go to a party with me after a basketball game. What a mistake that was! She looked down at me, with a big smile on her face, picked me up in her arms and started running across campus with me in her arms, saying how cute she thought I was.

My next and final fiasco with dating came when a buddy of mine who owned a little 1932 Chevy coupe with a rumble seat, talked two girls into going to the beach, Pacific Ocean Park (POP) with us. They agreed and off we went. Me and my date in the rumble seat. I felt really cool about having a honest-to-goodness, bona fide date!

We arrived at the beach and began playing some of the games, trying to win prizes. I wanted to show how good I was at these games, although I had never played them before. I didn't win a thing.

Next we decided on riding the roller-coaster and the girls were scared and doubtful about riding on it. We assured them it was not that big of a deal, not that scary at all. I didn't know if my buddy had been on a roller coaster before, but I knew I hadn't. Still, I played the big, brave hero, telling my date not to worry, I would protect her.

We purchased our tickets and were ushered to our little metal cars and strapped in. The cars began with a jerk and started moving slowly along the tracks. My date was still showing how scared she was. This gave me the opportunity to put my arm around her and tell her not to worry, "Hold onto me, I'll protect you!" The cars started rattling up the tracks very slowly while I continually reassured her she would be just fine. I also thought this would be nothing to get excited about as it slowly came closer to the top.

When we finally reached the top, I looked down and saw no tracks, just a straight drop with no end in sight. Our car began plunging downward at such speed, I was certain it had jumped the tracks and we were falling. I was scared out of my mind, let go of my date and put my head in her lap while wrapping my arms around her knees. I was never so scared of anything in my life and was hoping the ride would end right away. I couldn't get my breath as the car kept shaking and rising and falling, twisting and turning for what seemed like an eternity. When the ride was finally over, I was shaking like a leaf and had to go to the bathroom immediately. My date and the other couple laughed at me all the way home. Whenever I saw her at school after that night, I would drop my head and go another way.

I was equally as interested in music as I was in art and enrolled in the school choir, but was turned down because my voice was changing. I was a second soprano and was told if I sang now, it would ruin my voice. The choir director told to come back next semester and it should be okay. I returned each semester and was still unable to join, my voice kept changing and was told I would probably have a pretty low voice in the end. So I never sang in high school.

During my senior year, our art teacher, Ms. Sargent, informed us that the Walt Disney Studios in Burbank, California was offering an opportunity for graduating Los Angeles high school students to submit portfolios of their work to the studio for evaluation and a possible chance for employment there after graduation. We were encouraged to prepare our portfolios to be submitted. I was ecstatic about this opportunity. My imagination was working overtime. I envisioned being a cartoonist for Walt Disney, who was also from Kansas City, and I was certain that once he saw my artwork and found out I was from Kansas City too, he would hire me immediately. I wasted no time getting my portfolio organized, even drawing a few Disney characters for good measure.

The portfolios were submitted for review and returned after a few weeks, revealing which ones were accepted or rejected. When we came to class, Mrs. Sargent told those of us who had submitted our portfolios how proud she was of us, even the ones who were not accepted. She opened a folder and began reading the names of those who had been accepted. I was sitting on the edge of my seat, with sweaty palms and itchy, wet armpits.

The names were read off alphabetically and my last name being White, I had to sweat it out until she reached the end of the list. Lo and behold, she called out, "Robert White." YES!! I was in, I made it! I couldn't wait to tell my Mother and Mr. Venerable. I was beside myself. I barely heard her telling us the date and all the details surrounding our interviews at the studio.

It was a Monday morning, two weeks after getting the news, the five of us who were accepted were on the streetcar heading to The Disney Studios in Burbank, with our portfolios tucked tightly under our arms. Upon arriving, we noticed students from other schools entering the office lobby. We filed in right behind them and signed in at the front desk. Everybody was very excited, talking and laughing nervously amongst themselves. The room was filled with about fifteen boys and girls awaiting their big opportunity to start their careers as cartoonists or animators for Walt Disney.

While sitting with my fellow art students, I heard a female voice call out my name, "Robert White, would you come to the front desk, please?" My friends were so excited for me saying, "Ooh, Robert, you're going to be interviewed first. I'm not surprised, you're soo good!" Words of encouragement were given me, "Go get 'em Robert!" "Good luck, man!"

Nervously, I weaved my way through the few standing students and came to the desk where a brown-haired, middle-aged woman, looking very officious in her horn-rimmed glasses, looked at me sympathetically, and said, "Robert, I am so sorry, but you will not be able to be interviewed for a position because we do not hire any Negroes!" I was unable to speak and would not have known what to say anyway. I just stood there with my mouth open, sweat beginning to come out on my forehead, trying to handle what she had just told me. Finally, I think I said something like, "Uhh, okay," turned and started what seemed like a long walk back through the students, standing around, head down, not making eye contact with anyone. Not until then did I become aware that I was the only black person in the room. It seemed like I would never get back to where my friends were sitting, nor did I want to.

They observed me making my way back, not to where they were, but toward the front door. Just before I reached the door, a couple of them came over to me and grabbed my arm, when they saw my saddened face. "Robert, what happened? You didn't get interviewed?" I told them no, I would not be given an interview, and too embarrassed to say why not. They would not accept my not giving them a reason as to why not, and kept pressing me for an answer. Finally, I told them the Disney Company does not hire black people. They stood there dumbfounded and shocked with their mouths open as I walked out of the door with tears now beginning to well up in my eyes.

I had never experienced discrimination before and it left me hurt and very confused. I knew it existed in Missouri but I was never confronted with it so directly. I just did not expect anything like this in California. I went to school with kids of all ethnic backgrounds, ate in restaurants with everyone, went to movies and played with them. No difference was ever made. Why this? I walked to the streetcar stop, sat on the bench crying and wondering how could I face my mother, Mr. Venerable, my teacher and all the students in my class. I was so disappointed and sorry I entered my portfolio. Now what do I do? I would be graduating from high school in a few months and this was going to be my big chance at an art career. I thought, if companies discriminate against hiring black people, I will not become an artist after all. I'll just quit school and join the armed services like so many guys I knew had done. I discussed it with my mother and strangely enough, she didn't discourage me from joining. I was seventeen and she agreed to sign for me to enlist. It helped when I told her I would be sending her a monthly allotment check each month to help out around the house. She could use the extra help.

My art teacher, Ms. Sargent, tried to dissuade me from quitting school, she believed there was a future for me in art, regardless of the Disney incident. I was still very angry and disillusioned with art and had all but quit drawing, except for school assignments. Mr. Venerable had become very busy establishing new businesses after returning the hotels to their original owner and had little time for me and my problems. I was now focusing on joining the navy since several guys from school had joined and came home on leave in their dress blue Navy uniforms. I was very impressed with the uniform and enjoyed hearing them talk of foreign countries they had traveled to. I was hooked!

One day after school, I went down to the recruiting office to talk with the recruiting officer. I told him I was seventeen but, my mother agreed to sign the enlistment papers. He asked when did I want to enlist. I told him as soon as possible. Rubbing his chin, he stepped back and took a long look at me from head to toe, then asked, "How tall are you?" "I don't know!" I replied. "How much do you weigh?" Again, I answered, "I don't know." Walking away, he told me to follow him, which I did. We came to a stop at a set of weighing scales located in the corner of the room. "Take your shoes off and step up here!" he ordered. After getting on the scales, he brought a metal measuring stick down until it touched the top of my head. I stood there, looking at him, and waiting for the results of the weigh-in. He stepped back and said, "Well son, you are not big enough to join the Navy. You need to be at least five feet tall and weigh no less than one-hundred and five pounds. You are four-foot eleven inches tall and weigh one-hundred and two pounds! You need to grow some more. Come back in a few months and we will check you again."

Once more, I was beyond being pissed off. I thought, What the hell can I do in life? I can't become an artist because I am black and I can't change that, and I can't join the Navy because I am too damned little. I stood there frozen and angry, not hearing all he was saying to me. Finally he put his hand on my shoulder and I heard him say, "When you come back, eat as many bananas as you can and stand up all the way down here, okay?"

As a result of me being to small to enlist, I stayed in school and graduated. However, my desire to enlist never waned. I was going to be a sailor in the United States Navy.

I spent the summer working with a handy man Mr. Venerable had hired to paint and do general upkeep of several rooming houses he had purchased.

During the first part of September, I decided to go back to the Navy enlistment office to see if I qualified to join now. I sure hoped so because I had been bragging to all my friends that I would be leaving for the Navy soon. The morning I chose to go, I gorged down four or five bananas, boarded the streetcar which took me directly to city hall, where I walked into the recruiting office. The same officer was there, remembered me and said, "Oh you're back to try it again, huh? Hold it right there!" He got up from his desk, walked over to me, picked me up and told me to hang from the entrance door jam as long as I could. I did as he told me and dropped down to the floor after about a minute or so. "Okay, c'mon over and check in at the scales!" I walked over, took off my shoes and stepped on the scales, standing as straight as a rod. He began his measurements and when he had finished, he stepped back quickly. Clapped his hands and said, "Well, I'll be damned, you made it, sailor!" I weighed in at one-hundred seven and had grown two inches.

After having passed the height and weight test, I was scheduled for a physical exam the following week. My enlistment was now becoming a reality. Mom asked me repeatedly if this was what I wanted to do. I assured her it was, and more importantly, provided me an opportunity to be of some financial assistance to her. She was working long hours and for not much money as a maid at Mr. Venerable's hotels.

The week passed quickly and I was back at the recruiting center for my physical along with a lot of other guys. We were ordered to strip down to our underwear, after which a team of naval doctors checked us over from head to toe. Immediately, I thought about what mom had told us all our lives, "Always have on clean underwear just in case you are in an accident." Mine was clean and had no holes in it.

Four hours later, it was over and we were told we could get dressed. We reported back into the waiting room, and given the results of our exams. I felt relieved and glad that I had passed with flying colors! Now on to the next step - becoming a sailor.

On the morning of October 18,1948, I, and about twenty other guys, were loaded into a dark blue bus with big white letters that read, UNITED STATES NAVY on each side. We were taken to a naval reserve training location on the outskirts of Los Angeles and herded into a large empty building where only a podium stood with the American flag posted on one side and the California State flag on the other.

Immediately, a heavyset guy wearing U.S. the Navy dress blue uniform stepped upon the podium. His uniform had several rows of colorful campaign ribbons pinned on the upper left side of his uniform jumper. On each of his sleeves were three red, v-shaped stripes and a white eagle above them. I later learned this signified his rank. He was a first class petty officer and the three short red slashes on the lower part of his right uniform sleeve signified how long he had been in the Navy. Each slash, called hash marks, represented four years of service.

Once on the podium, he turned and faced us, then in a loud voice, he shouted out, "Alright recruits, knock off the grab-assing, line up in two rows and come to attention! You are about to become proud members of the finest organization in this country, The United States Navy! I am going to swear you in and once I have completed that, you then become property of the United States Navy!"

SAN DIEGO, CALIFORNIA

My first weeks of boot camp consisted of being issued all my clothing, toilet articles and receiving all the necessary shots I needed. Getting the shots was quite a shock for me. We all stood in line, (which I found out would be routine for everything we did for the next four years), wearing nothing but our skivvies (shorts and undershirt), awaiting our turn to get these most dreaded shots in the arm. But there was one shot we all were dreading; the one, sailors who had been in camp for a longer time, told us new recruits it would be given with a square-tipped needle and injected into your left testicle.

As I got closer there were corpsmen on each side of the line giving the shots and asking each guy where they were from. If the guy said he was from a state the corpsman liked or was from, he smiled and injected the needle with more compassion. If it was a state he didn't care for, he seemed to stick the needle with force. When my turn came and was asked what state I was from, I replied California. The corpsmen looked at the other one on the opposite side and said, "Oh, boy! We got one here from the land of fruits and nuts!" They jammed the needles into my arms at the same time with no degree of compassion and told me,

Seaman Recruit Robert White, U.S.N.

"Move out, sailor!" I never knew what that was about, but found out later. I could hardly lift my arms for the next couple of days.

We were referred to as "Boots" or "Recruits" and green as grass. We believed any and everything the more seasoned guys told us. Consequently, we became the butt end of many practical jokes. One of my first evenings on base, I was standing in this ever-so-long chow line that stretched outside the chow hall, waiting patiently as the line snaked its way towards the chow hall entrance. Eventually, I got inside the door, picked up my food tray and utensils, when a guy behind the serving line yelled out at me, "Sailor, have you had your food tray stenciled?" Turning the tray over in my hands, I told him, "No sir, I don't think I have." "Then, you've got to have that tray stenciled before you can eat on it!" I looked at him dumbfounded, saying nothing. He continued, "Get out of line, sailor, and take that tray across the grinder (the marching field) to the sick bay and get it stenciled. Double time, you got that?" I said, "Yes sir," got out of line and began trotting double time across the long field to the medical building. When I got there, puffing and blowing, I walked in holding my tray up in front of me and told the corpsman I was there to have my tray stenciled. He looked at me and broke out laughing loudly, telling me someone played a practical joke on me, no one stencils trays before they eat. Feeling really stupid and angry, I headed back across the field to the chow hall, but when I arrived, the Master-at-Arms met me at the door and told me the chow line had closed. I placed the tray on the stack of other trays and left. I went without dinner that day.

Some time later when I was first stationed aboard ship and not knowing my way around, I was told by my First Class Petty Officer to go to the tool crib a bring him a sky hook. Naively, I returned to report they did not have one in stock.

485 was the number of my company which consisted of about forty guys, seemingly from every state in the union. I was assigned the duty of Guide on Bearer. My job was to carry the company flag in front of the company whenever we marched anywhere on base or were in a parade. It made me very proud to be out front of the company carrying our flag. It was also my duty to get the mail and distribute it.

One day we were in a training class observing a film that taught us the names of different parts of a ship. When the narrator of the film came to one part of the ship, he gave the proper name for it then said, it was commonly called a "Nigger Head." I heard a couple of guys seated behind me start to laugh softly and one said, "Here's a couple of nigger heads in front of us." My buddy sitting next to me asked me if I heard what he had said. I told him I did, and since I had to leave class early to pick up the mail, I would meet him in the barracks and kick his butt.

I left the training class and walked angrily across the grounds to the post office, picked up the mail and met the company inside our barracks. Everyone approached me asking if they had mail. I went through the mail, tossing letters to each guy as I read his name. Whenever I came across a letter for the guy who had pissed me off by calling us nigger heads, I put it behind the others. When I had finished, I started walking towards the restroom (the head), calling out the offender's name, telling him he had mail and to follow me to the head. I walked in through the swinging doors and stood just inside them. As he approached the door, pushing it open, I reached out, grabbing him by the collar and pulled him in. "I'll teach you to call me a Nigger Head," and threw a punch hitting him squarely on the jaw, jamming his head against the door frame. He shook his head several times then started coming at me. He began punching me so hard, I couldn't see as I flailed at him with both fists and my eyes closed. We fought all across the restroom, through the urinals, wash basins and into the showers. I was clearly getting the worst of it and wished I had never started it. I ended up being hit in the eye as I landed on the toilet. He stood up over me and told me, as far as he was concerned, I was still a Nigger Head and walked out. I had never been in a real fight, this was my first and I lost it badly. However, I learned a lesson; you can't beat up everyone who calls you a derogatory name.

During my three months in boot camp, I began to grow. I grew so much the uniforms I was issued were too small and I had to be issued a larger size in everything. By the time I finished boot camp, I was five foot eight inches tall and weighed one hundred and thirty-five pounds. When I went home on leave, I rang the doorbell at our house and my mother opened the door. Momentarily, she did not recognize me. When she did, she threw her arms around my neck and said, "Oh, My God! Just look at you! You're so tall!" I continued to grow until I reached the height of six feet at age 22.

MEMPHIS, TENNESSEE

After completing boot camp, I applied to attend Aviation Store-keeper School in Millington, Tennessee, a naval training center just outside of Memphis. I had never been in the deep south before and was somewhat naïve as to just how prejudiced people were and how segregated life was for black people. There were four of us who were reporting for school and I was the only black. We knew each other well and boarded the train in San Diego eagerly, looking forward to our six months of training. The Navy had provided us with meal tickets throughout the trip, but on the morning the train pulled in to the Memphis station, we had not used our last meal ticket. The conductor told us it would be honored in the station and we could have our breakfast there.

The four of us entered the station and went right into the restaurant and presented our meal tickets to the cashier. In a heavy southern drawl, he spoke, telling us yes we could use the tickets there, then added, "But the boy will have to go round behind the baggage room to eat!" Being from California, none of us were certain as to what he meant.

One of the guys questioned him as to what he meant. Irritated, he looked at us and said, "The three of you can eat in here, but him (pointing his finger close to my face), he can't eat in here!" The guys were shocked and one told him, "Sir, we are in the United States Navy, we're reporting for duty here. We're all together!" Irritated, he replied, "I don't give a damn who you are and what you are doing. You are in the South now, and the boy can't eat in here!" They turned and looked at me and said, "Well, if you can't eat in here, we won't eat in here either! We'll all eat with you behind the baggage room!" "Naw, y'all ain't allowed back there. The sign says, for colored only!"

Embarrassed, I broke out in sweat all over, which I usually do, and told them it would be okay, I would meet up with them after breakfast. I walked out and around the corner to the entrance of the baggage room. Entering, I noticed a large area where porters were sorting piles of luggage and on the other side of the room was a lunch counter with four or five stools. Behind the counter was a heavyset white waitress serving food to a couple of customers. I took a seat and looked at the tattered and dirty menu as the waitress came over and asked me what I was having. I told her bacon and eggs, over medium, wheat toast and coffee. She wrote it down and placed it on a ledge in a small opening that connected to the kitchen where orders were prepared and placed on the opening to be served to the black customers.

I waited for about forty-five minutes before my order was filled and placed on the ledge. When she finally served it to me, it was so cold, the grease around the eggs had hardened and turned white. The toast was burnt and hard. I tried to eat it but, couldn't. I drank the coffee, gave her my meal ticket and left.

This incident, and many others that I experienced over the course of the six months I spent there caused me to realize, I was in the south and had to adjust to the their ways of doing things. Being in the Navy made no difference. I would just do what I had to do, graduate and get my butt back to California.

SAN FRANCISCO, CALIFORNIA

I graduated and received orders shipping me out to a temporary base in San Francisco for FFT (For Further Transfer). I was so glad to get back to California I did not care where I was going to be transferred to, as long as it was north of the Mason-Dixon Line.

After spending two weeks there assigned to work details, mess cooking in the galley, swabbing floors, cleaning bulkheads (walls) in the barracks. I got out of some of the details drawing pin-up girls for the petty officers to put up on the walls of their offices. Eventually, my orders came through assigning me to an aircraft carrier, the Phillipine Sea, CV-47.

My ship pulled into port and I was amazed at its size. The crew consisted of three thousand five hundred men, not including the pilots. When I reported onboard and settled into my compartment, I went back up on deck looking down nearly three stories at all the families with children being held by sailors as they said their good-byes; couples hugging, kissing and shedding tears, on the docks. I was still standing there when the ship began pulling away from the docks. The crowd of people were waving goodbye to their loved ones onboard. I watched the people get smaller and smaller as we drifted farther out into the bay, guided by a couple of small tugboats on either side of our gigantic craft.

I had never been aboard a ship before, so this was pretty exciting for me, until we were out beyond the three-mile limit. Suddenly the ship started to swaying slowly from side to side. I started feeling woozy and my stomach became upset. I knew I was going to be sick so I ran from the deck down to the first head I could make it to. Once there, I threw up everything I had eaten. Leaving the head, I staggered from side to side as I walked through the compartments, with the ship continuing to sway more violently. I reached my compartment, fell onto my bunk and stayed there the rest of the afternoon battling seasickness.

A couple of days later, I found my sea legs and became acclimated to life aboard this big floating hotel. There was lots of activity onboard to keep us occupied after duty hours. We had a Gedunk Stand where you could buy all sorts of goodies; soft drinks, malts, candy, magazines and just about anything you wanted. My favorite spot was the afterdeck where musicians would gather and have jam sessions. I had the opportunity to sit-in and sing with them.

After spending fifty-five days at sea, we were glad when we docked in Yokosuka, Japan on a ten-day stay and a chance to spread our wings in the city; no need to expound on "spreading our wings." We left Japan and went to Korea for about the same amount of time and more wing spreading. (I don't remember if we went to Japan or Korea first.)

Our tour lasted six months, and we returned to the states. During that time, I put in a request to be transferred to Special Services at North Island in San Diego. I made it a point to become acquainted with the guy in charge of the Special Services unit, Buddy Viotti, a very talented pianist who sang, played jazz accordion and arranged all the music. I wanted to be a part of this group badly. It seemed as though the transfer would never come through or even if it was going to be approved, so I continued aboard ship, doing tours and jamming on the aft deck.

Whenever we were docked in the San Francisco or San Diego areas, my buddies and I would go out on liberty; and since none of us had a lot of money to spend and what little we had, we'd spend so quickly, leaving us more time than we had money. I came up with a scheme to possibly pick up a little spending money. I suggested we seek out theaters that put on talent shows which I would sign up for. I would come out and sing my song with my buddies in the audience. When the time came to judge the winner, usually the judge would walk along the contestants holding his hand over the heads of each of us. The audience would clap and yell for their favorite and the one who received the most applause and the loudest yelling would be declared the winner. Well, needless to say, when the judge held his hand over my head, my partially drunk sailor buddies would stomp, clap, scream and yell so loudly and long, that I was instantly declared the winner. First prize was usually twenty-five dollars. I would collect my prize money and leave with my buddies, split the winnings and proceed to party again. This happened a few times before the manager of the theater got wise and would not let me enter. However, in San Diego, the manager of the theater made me the master of ceremonies of the talent show and I got paid twenty bucks a week for as long as my ship was in port.

We were somewhere in the middle of the Pacific Ocean when the Personnel Officer called me to his office and informed me my transfer had been approved for Special Services and I would be transferred back to the states immediately. I wondered how this would be possible since we were in the middle of the raging sea. I soon found out. I packed my sea bag and was ordered to report to the hangar deck at 0800 hours the following morning. I did so, and there at one of the large openings, where the deck crew took on supplies, was a huge wooden box painted Navy gray, with one end opened. There were several other sailors standing there beside me, sea bags in tow, waiting to be transferred also. Shortly, a naval tanker, used for carrying fuel, pulled alongside. It sat so low in the ocean you could barely see the deck. To make matters worse, the sea was tossing both ships up and down very violently. I understood now this was our transportation back to the states. Getting aboard with such a violent, turbulent sea was the problem. As the ships came in close proximity, a large steel cable was suddenly shot across the waters to the tanker. The box had a steel cable attached to a big pulley on top. We were told to enter the box for transfer to the tanker. We entered, and the end of the box was secured, and off we went, out the ship's opening into the angry sea that kept rising and falling with each big wave. We were gliding back and forth between the two ships with each swell of the big waves. Once we got close and deck hands would reach out to pull us in, the ship would toss in the opposite direction sending us back the other way. After nearly forty-five minutes, we reached the deck of the tanker. I was twenty years of age at the time and did not recognize the danger we faced in the middle of that big, turbulent ocean. (As I look back on it today, it scares the hell out of me.)

SAN DIEGO, CALIFORNIA

Once back in San Diego, I reported for duty at North Island Naval Air Station, then to my Special Services unit located in the base theater where I met the other fifteen members of unit; musicians, singers, comedians and writers. Buddy took me to a backstage office and explained the duties we were to perform and of other responsibilities. We reported to a lieutenant in charge of the Special Services Department. This included all the sports teams, Community Services and all activities involving the theater. Our regular duty, between USO shows and other on base entertainment, was to open and close the theater before and after the movie. We also had the responsibility of taking tickets and cleaning the theater. During

Relaxing backstage after completion of show with Bob Hope.

the day, we spent our time around the piano with Buddy teaching us new songs, and ones he had made special arrangements of for our next show. When Buddy had written a new show, we rehearsed it all day. Once completed, we performed them in local theaters around town. Other times, we performed our shows in local parking lots throughout the city, from a flat-bed truck. Our shows were very entertaining. We had absolutely hilarious comedy skits and great music. Our main comedian and master of ceremonies was

Skip Young, who became a big star and regular on the Ozzie and Harriet television show.

The highlight of my two years assigned to Special Services was when well-known personalities put on shows at our base and other bases in California, they would include us in their shows, performing with them. There was Jack Benny and my favorite, Bob Hope. They would provide us small comedy bits to perform with them. I had a relatively big skit I performed with Bob Hope where I was a shore patrol officer who had to arrest him for being an AWOL sailor. I came on stage grabbing him by his coat collar and the seat of his pants while ushering him offstage with him protesting I had the wrong guy, he was classified as 4F. I returned later in the show and sang a solo. Mr. Hope was very nice and while he and I were seated backstage, he told me I had a good voice and to stick with it. That bit of encouragement sustained me for many periods when I wanted to quit trying for a career in show business.

October 18, 1952, I was honorably discharged at North Island Naval Base in San Diego, California. I was a happy guy, ready to set the world of show business on its ear with my singing. The few successes I had under my belt and a degree of popularity, had caused me to become a bit cocky. I started believing my own publicity. Nothing could stop me now. Move over Sinatra, Nat Cole, Billy Eckstine, Tony Bennett and everybody else, make room for Bob White!

It was a bright, sunny day when I walked towards the guard gate with my discharge papers in hand. I approached the gate and showed my papers to the marine on duty. He looked over the papers and waved me through. Cockily, I shouted, "I am a civilian again, I am free of the Navy," and threw my white hat into a body of water that flowed under the small bridge at the gate. The guard yelled, "Come back here sailor, and go get that hat, or you're going to the brig for destroying government issued property!" I told him I was no longer in the Navy, I am discharged. Forcefully, he shouted back, "Look at your papers, it says you are still in the Navy until 2400 hours, twelve midnight!"

Embarrassed, I took off my shoes and socks, rolled up my uniform pant legs and waded out to retrieve my white hat. As I picked it up, the guard told me to put it on my head. Grumbling under my breath, I did so and waded out of the water and off the base.

I have to admit the many pitfalls, road blocks and meager beginnings I had to contend with, the disappointments, rejections and bad decisions, dampened my spirits at times, but fortunately, none of it affected my desire to accomplish something in my life. I would not end up a drunk like my father, as my mother often told me I would.

LOS ANGELES, CALIFORNIA

While in the Navy, I drew cartoons that were published in the Our Navy Magazine. After being discharged, I enrolled at Los Angeles City College under the G.I. Bill, majoring in commercial art and music as a minor. I also found the time to get married.

The girl I married was a good friend of an ex-girlfriend of mine. We hit it off quite well in the beginning. (By this time in my life, I had grown to a normal height and weight and with four years of the Navy under my belt, my self-confidence was running high and I was quite sure of myself where the girls were concerned. I developed a witty personality and kept everyone laughing, especially, the girls.) She had a great sense of humor and I kept her laughing. Unfortunately, the laughing stopped when she informed me she was pregnant. Understandably, she was quite upset and didn't know how to handle the situation. I told her not to worry, we'd just get married and raise the child.

We ran off to Tijuana, Mexico and got married, returned and rented a little house. I now needed a job to supplement my G.I. Bill check to take care of my wife and soon-to-be-born child. I began working at Chrysler's Car Assembly Plant and started attending school at night. This was working out well until my wife gave birth to our little daughter. Two weeks after giving birth, she was diagnosed

One of my first gigs in an L.A. nightclub.

with Post-Partum Depression, and after a court hearing, the judge decided she needed mental care. She was placed in the Camarillo State Hospital for a period of three months, and underwent regular electrical shock treatments. I was lost. Here I was with a new baby, which I knew nothing of how to care for, trying to hold down a job and attend college at night.

Something had to give, so it was my college classes. I took a two-week leave of absence from Chrysler to adjust to this new and foreign life I had to live. I was left alone with a newborn baby that I barely knew how to hold, let alone care for. Luckily, my mother and sisters came to my rescue and took turns at helping me with the baby, and gave me a crash course in changing diapers (no Pampers at that time), mixing formula, burping and overall infant care. I believe without their help, I would have been in Camarillo Hospital, too.

We were married for over ten years. During that time, she had periodic stays in the mental hospital and there were two more children born, my son and another daughter.

Throughout those years, I continued my music, performing at weddings, afternoon teas, in church choirs and in local nightclubs. It was while doing a guest appearance in a local nightclub that I was approached by Paul Robi, an original member of The Platters vocal group, who told me they were looking for someone to replace the baritone singer with the group. He said he liked my voice, thought I would make a good replacement and would I consider becoming a member of the group. I didn't know if he was serious or not, so I didn't give him an answer at that time. I knew who The Platters were, a Doo-Wop group, but I was not into that kind of music. I never sang in a group before and knew none of their 16 golden hit records. I was a soloist, a crooner like Billy Eckstine, Nat Cole, Frank Sinatra and other big band singers. He told me he was very serious and wanted my telephone number. We exchanged numbers then he left saying he would call me in a day or so to find out my decision. After a couple of days thinking about it and discussing it with my wife, we agreed it might be good for us financially.

So I agreed to sign a contract with the group.

Within a couple of weeks I had obtained my passport and was off on a tour of the Orient as a member of The World Famous Platters Vocal Group.

We left Los Angeles International Airport on a ten-and-a-half hour non-stop flight to Tokyo, Japan. Flying that long was to be the first of many new experiences for me. I had flown on Navy planes for short periods of time around San Diego but never this long. When we arrived in Tokyo and the plane was taxiing up to the terminal, to my utter surprise, Platters music began playing over the intercom on the plane. The airline attendants were talking and nodding amongst themselves, and looking at us with smiles on their faces. Evidently, they knew throughout the trip who we were but never let on that they were aware of it. We were treated the same as everyone else on the plane. The passengers, mostly Japanese, waited in their seats as the attendants beckoned for us to come forward to deplane. As we walked up the aisle toward the exit, they began applauding softly as we passed by. I have to admit, that was a very special moment for me. My first exposure to star treatment.

In the terminal, we were met by our Japanese promoter and his several assistants who promptly ushered us into a waiting stretch limousine that rapidly maneuvered its way through heavy traffic on the downtown streets of Tokyo. During the trip, the promoter spoke to the driver, evidently instructing him to pull over and park. After doing so, and the promoter turned, looked back at us with a big smile while pointing up at a very tall building, and then said in broken English, "Excuse me, but please, look up at the top of this building to see our company's promotion of your tour!" We craned our necks out of the windows, and up at the top of this tall building, there across the roof were ten to fifteen-foot, wooden cutout images of the five of us, with "The Platters" written behind our heads. I was completely flabbergasted! The promoter broke out in uncontrolled laughter as he enjoyed seeing the surprise on my face. I'm certain it was old hat to the original members of the group but for me, the expression on my face said it all. I was still looking out the rear window at it as we drove off. It was my intention to take a picture of it but never did.

After settling in to our hotel, we were given an itinerary listing performance dates, times and rehearsals. I noticed our first rehearsal was scheduled for the next morning with our first two shows scheduled that same evening. This made me very nervous because I knew I would need more rehearsals to learn my part and especially, the choreography because I had two left feet, a lousy dancer! I went immediately to Zola's room and told her of my concern. Again, she smiled, telling me, "You'll be fine, no need to worry."

Mid-morning, the next day we were met in the lobby by another smiling assistant and escorted to our limo and transported to the concert hall. Once inside, there were a multitude of musicians assembling onstage (I had never sang with more than five). I later learned it was a thirty-two piece orchestra. Our pianist and musical arranger presented our music to the orchestra leader and we took our places onstage. Now I'm sweating bullets and thinking, "Here you are in a foreign country, getting ready to sing and don't know what the hell you are going to sing or do! How did I allow this to happen? What's more, its too damned late to get out of it now!" I am sweating under my arms as I usually do when I am nervous and to make matters worse, I think I need to pee. I wondered if I could tell them to hold on a minute while I go pee.

Well, fortunately for me, I stand next to Zola in the line-up, so I frantically say to her, "Zola! You know I don't know what to do. I'm going to screw it up!" Calmly, she looked me in the eye and quietly said to me, "Here is what you do. I want you to hold onto my thumb during each song. If I move my thumb up, you take the note up higher, If I move it down, you take it down. If it doesn't change, keep singing the same note!"

That evening we were standing in place onstage behind a heavy drawn curtain, dressed in our tailor-made black tuxedos and Zola in a long, form-fitting gold sequined gown waiting for the orchestra to finishing the opening refrain of "Only You," then introduce us.

Suddenly, the theater went dark, the curtain began slowly rising and a thunderous voice speaking a few words in Japanese, then in broken English, I understood him to say, "The World Famous Platters!" Spotlight beams darted back and forth, up and down throughout the theater revealing hundreds of faces in the audience applauding continuously, while the house lights were turned up. I could feel my heart pounding as loudly as the bass drum when suddenly, I heard Paul Robi say, "Okay, let's do it!" I reached and found Zola's thumb and held on for dear life as we went into "Only You." I released it briefly when we took our bows, but found it quickly before starting each song during our hour-long show.

Believe it or not, it worked! My first two concerts with the Platters, in front of hundreds of people were performed with me being directed by a thumb! We were a huge success, receiving standing ovations and bouquets of flowers after each show. Upon exiting the theater, it was a common practice for young female fans to wait

Johnny K. (lead guitarist in our band), myself and Zola being greeted in China after a long, sleepless flight.

Backstage after the show for a photo-shoot and news release (the young girl with pigtails is Paul Robi's daughter, who is now the wife of boxing champ Sugar Ray Leonard).

outside the exit for us to throw our bow ties to them. We replaced a lot of bow ties.

Our three-month tour of the Orient included performances in China and Thailand. When it was over, I had become acclimated pretty well to life on the road, the notoriety that went along with being a Platter. Still I was the "Rookie" of the group and was subjected to all that "Rooks" have to endure. In short, I was the "Gofer" Go for this, go for that.

One Gofer duty I performed on a regular basis was getting our mail and distributing it when we were booked in a venue for a period of time. There was one occasion when I collected the mail that stands out above all the rest. We were booked in the Newport Hotel in Miami, Florida for three weeks. I reported to the front desk faithfully each morning, picked up the mail and distributed it. One morning during the last week of our engagement, I stood

at the front desk, engaged in conversation with the desk clerk as he sorted the mail. Suddenly, he turned, looked past me and with a big smile and surprised look on his face said, "Good morning Little Richard! Welcome to the Newport Hotel!" I turned and looked directly into his heavily-made up face that was partially hidden by big, dark sunglasses, with white sequined frames. Immediately, he began talking fast and non-stop as he greeted the desk clerk, completely ignoring my presence. I could not believe what I was seeing! Such flamboyant attire; a very wide-brimmed white hat with one side turned down which he wore cocked to one side, a fur-collared, waist length white cape covering a white satin long-sleeved shirt, white pants with sequins running up the seams and white patent-leather boots. My disbelief led me to think how could anyone wear such outrageously, gaudy clothing in public. Hell, it was way over the top to be worn on stage. He made Liberace look conservative.

My gaze was interrupted by the desk clerk saying, "Oh, by the way Little Richard, this is Bob White, a member of the Platters!" With a

With The Platters in Buenos Aires, Argentina

No! I am not yawning!

look of pleasant surprise and the typical, phony show-biz smile, he removed his sunglasses, laid them on the desk, looked at me and in a louder than normal voice said to me, "Oh my goodness Baby Boy, how nice to meet you!" Before I could react or answer, he reached out with both hands, cupped my cheeks and quickly kissed me on the mouth! I never saw it coming, I stood there frozen, shocked, dumbfounded, and couldn't believe what had just happened.

He reached out, took the key to his suite while thanking the clerk and pranced off through the lobby. As he walked he was saying something to me about telling Paul and Zola to be sure and come to the party he always throws in his suite on his first night in town. The reality of what had just occurred was beginning to set in for me as I stood there continually wiping my mouth off. The next emotion I was experiencing was one of being thoroughly pissed off. I noticed the clerk look over at me with a slight smile then quickly looked down as I stared at him not too pleasantly. After all these years, I still reflect back on that unpleasant moment and see

POR PRIMERA VEZ EN SANTIAGO

Creadores de
"Mi Oración"
"Sólo Tú"
"El toque mágico"
"Tres monedas en
la fuente"
y muchas otras.

'THE PLATTERS'

Famoso Conjunto Mundial

TEATRO "ASTOR"

3 y 4 de Marzo
19,15 y 22 hrs
Unicos recitales extraordinarios

Reserva de entradas en Boletería del Teatro

TRANSMISION EXCLUSIVA de RADIO CORPORACION

Advertisement from newspaper in Santiago, Chile.

that mask of a face, with the little, thin mustache pressing against my mouth and cringe.

It was the late sixties and the early seventies; new artists and new styles of dress had come on the scene. The most popular artist to invade the pop charts was a young, handsome, curly-haired Welsh singer from Pontypridd, South Wales, named Tom Jones. He topped the charts with his recordings of "What's New Pussycat," "Delilah," and many others. He possessed a big, powerful baritone voice that appealed to the listening public, male and female alike. However, he had one quality that appealed to the female population as much, if not more than his voice. It was the skin-tight bell-bottomed pants he wore and his sexual gyrations while performing. He drove the women in the audience into a frenzy night after night causing them to throw their bras and panties at him onstage.

Tight-fitting bell-bottomed trousers and platform shoes were the rage for young men and women during this period in time. Consequently, it was only a matter of time before The Platters updated their mode of dress to include the new look. Our tuxedos and dinner jackets became double-breasted with much tighter bell-bottomed pants. We also branched out into more casual outfits that included loose-fitting, open-collared shirts.

Our act usually included a musical comedy skit or two in each of our shows, so, to stay current with what was hot at the time, we built a skit based on Tom Jones' big hit, "Delilah." The song is about a woman named Delilah who is caught being unfaithful to her lover. In a fit of anger, he proceeds to slash her with a knife, after which he stands over her, questioning why. Being the baritone singer in the group, I was chosen to sing the song and one of the other guys would be Delilah. The skit began with me singing the song through completely, making Tom Jones-like gyrations. Suddenly, Delilah comes sauntering out wearing a red wig and a wrap-around dress. I walk towards her and swing as if to slash her with a knife in my hand. She falls down on stage and I straddle her singing, "My, my, my, Delilah, why, why, why, Delilah?"

The skit was always well received, bringing lots of laughter and applause so, we kept it in our act. However, as fate would have it, a mishap occurred during one of the performances, that caused me much embarrassment. We performed the skit wearing our skin-tight white bell bottomed trousers, loose-collared shirts worn over our pants and a long multi-colored sash around our waists. Unfortunately, we wore no underwear or briefs due to the tightness of our pants, as it would leave an unsightly line on our pants.

I started singing and gyrating and all was going fine until I threw my arm out to slash Delilah and she fell to the floor. When I stepped over and straddled her head, I heard a loud rip! I had split my pants in the crotch, exposing my privates. Fortunately, I was standing at an angle that no one in the audience could observe what had just happened.

The guy playing the part of Delilah had to look up at me through-out the rest of the skit. Later he told me he thought the damn song would never end.

Most people would think stardom and public adulation would be nice to experience. However, there can be negative aspects as well, which I found out. During one of our South American tours, we were scheduled to perform at an outdoor venue in Lima, Peru. The location was a flat open field, reminiscent in size of the Woodstock concert. As our limo came through the entrance, there were wall-to-wall people as far as the eye could see packed into this large open field, pulsating to the loud rhythms of a Latin band. Security guards surrounded our vehicle immediately, attempting to push back the crowd so we could drive through to the stage which was located in the middle of the field. As we inched our way along, there were people on all sides of the car, banging on it and rocking it from side to side. Their faces and hands were up against the win-dows, totally obscuring our view. I was afraid they would turn the car over. Even though we had the air conditioner on, it was getting hotter and hotter in that plush metal prison cell. I am extremely claustrophobic and was beginning to have a panic attack, feeling as though I could not breathe, and said so out loud. Paul told me to put my head between my legs and stay there until we reached the

THE PLATTERS

stage. I did, for what seemed like an eternity, until we reached the stage. So if any of you think that all aspects of being popular are cool, trust me, it's not. It's downright scary!

There were many memorable, fun-filled times that I experienced during my six years with the group. Yet there were others I choose not to remember. Traveling and living together for long periods of time throughout the year can become rather trying and frustrating. In essence, you are the same as a dysfunctional family living together, but must get along because you need each other. The situation became more complicated due to the replacing of personnel in the group, as you can see from the pictures. With each change came new personalities and egos that we had to adapt to, which was sometimes very challenging. There were instances when were

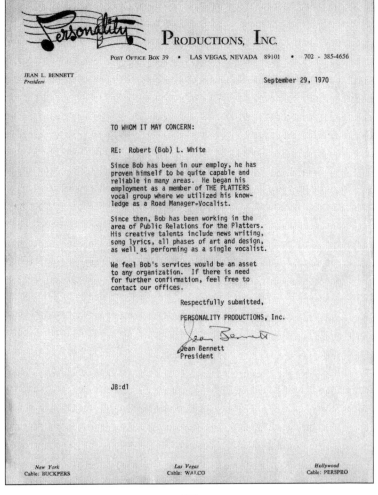

PRODUCTIONS, INC.

POST OFFICE BOX 39 • LAS VEGAS, NEVADA 89101 • 702 - 385-4656

JEAN L. BENNETT
President

September 29, 1970

TO WHOM IT MAY CONCERN:

RE: Robert (Bob) L. White

Since Bob has been in our employ, he has proven himself to be quite capable and reliable in many areas. He began his employment as a member of THE PLATTERS vocal group where we utilized his knowledge as a Road Manager-Vocalist.

Since then, Bob has been working in the area of Public Relations for the Platters. His creative talents include news writing, song lyrics, all phases of art and design, as well as performing as a single vocalist.

We feel Bob's services would be an asset to any organization. If there is need for further confirmation, feel free to contact our offices.

Respectfully submitted,

PERSONALITY PRODUCTIONS, Inc.

Jean Bennett
President

JB:dl

New York
Cable: BUCKPERS

Las Vegas
Cable: WALCO

Hollywood
Cable: PERSPRO

in the middle of big, heated arguments while waiting for the curtain to be opened. The moment it opened, the cursing stopped instantly, and ugly frowns turned into big smiles as we went into the opening number. After the show, whatever the argument was about was forgotten. After long periods on the road, it was not uncommon for us not to want to see each other when we returned home, until we had to.

To sum up my Platters years, I'd have to say they were most rewarding. I had the opportunity to make more money than I ever expected, buy a home, travel extensively, perform before dignitaries, heads of state and thousands of adoring fans. It was a learning experience, but one that had personal sacrifices.

My touring for those six years eventually took its toll on my marriage, resulting in my wife filing for divorce. Initially, I became aware of her intentions to divorce me when we returned home from a three month tour of South America. As we walked from the plane and into the terminal, there were family members greeting other members of the group and fans asking for autographs; none of my family was there. Amongst all the people and confusion, a guy asked rather loudly, "Which one of you is Bob White? Where is Bob White?" Giving no thought as to why he was asking for me, other than wanting an autograph, I answered by telling him I was Bob White. Hastily, he walked over to me and handed me a restraining order, restricting me from going home and I was not to come within fifty feet of the property.

I was totally shocked and somewhat confused. I knew my wife and I were going through some bad times before I left on tour. She and the kids did not come to the airport to see me off, as they usually did; she took them to a picnic instead. I went to a pay phone and called her to find out exactly what was going on. Sharply, she told me she was filing for divorce and not to call her anymore, talk with her lawyer instead. She closed the conversation with, "I am going to take the buttons off your shirt!"

Penniless and no place to stay, I bunked with a member of the group, temporarily. He spoke with his landlord and was told there was a little place I could rent very cheaply, located upstairs in the rear of the front house. I agreed and moved in right away. It consisted of a bedroom, tiny kitchen and bathroom. Jokingly, I called it My Penthouse. My friends referred to it as a Bird House. It was the smallest studio apartment I had ever seen. The bed was handmade and attached to one of the walls and so high, you had to really stretch your legs to climb in. Standing in the kitchen, with your arms outstretched, you could touch both walls. It was furnished with a small, four-burner stove with no oven and a tiny refrigerator. The bathroom was just as bad. There was no bath tub, only a small face bowl. My rent was twenty dollars a month and I ended up being months behind with that.

With all this drama in my life, I was constantly missing rehearsals with the group in preparation for our next tour of Europe. Our manager, Buck Ram, made the decision to replace me until all my legal problems were resolved. The show had to go on and it went on, without me.

She had emptied our joint bank account, leaving me broke. I was stuck with paying the mortgage and all the other bills, which were mostly delinquent because she refused to pay anything. At that time, if a contract had both our signatures on it, the husband was the one they went after to collect. (She got the mine and I got the shaft.)

It was during this period, out of absolute necessity, that I started making the rounds to small night clubs and restaurants inquiring about getting a gig there. I felt that having the years I spent with the Platters on my resume would be plus and open a door or two. It was quite nervy of me to promote myself so fervently when I did not have a band if I got hired. But I was ever so persistent and just knew, if I got the gig, I would find the necessary musicians. Its relatively common with musicians that, If you've got a gig, you can get a band but, guys are not much for wanting to rehearse if there is no gig. When owners told me they could not afford a band, I countered with, I will tailor the group to fit your budget, anything from a duo up. Additionally, I would provide an hour-long audition free. (Usually, I had to pay a small sum to the musicians.) On many occasions, they would allow us to audition, and afterwards tell me they would have to think about it and get back to me later. Most never got back, but they had just received an hour's worth of free entertainment. The jobs I did get, they liked the music we were playing. It was mostly for dancing and consisted of MOR music (Middle of the Road), soft rock, light jazz, standards, R&B and a medley of Platter tunes thrown in (since that was my claim to fame and advertised as being "Formerly of the Platters," it was expected).

Luckily, I did pick up a few jobs working weekends but, the pay was never much. Many nights we played to an empty house, which I worried about because I knew, more than likely, we were going to be let go. Other nights, our bar tabs amounted to more than we were making, so we ending up feeling good, but paying the house to work there. My luck changed when I landed a job on the Redondo Pier at the Polynesian Restaurant. The pay was better and we worked Thursday, Friday and Saturday night and Sunday afternoon with dinner included. I had a five-piece combo (piano, bass, drums, guitar and Congas). We were billed as, "Bob White (Formerly of The Platters) and The White House." They absolutely loved us there. Friday and Saturday nights, the place was packed, truly an adrenaline rush for musicians. Nothing better than playing for standing room only crowd. Initially, we were hired for six weeks, but it turned out to be an eighteen month engagement. I was still living in the "Bird Cage," and starting to see daylight in the mountain of bills I was buried under.

An incident occurred that I initially thought was going to create a problem in the band. Our keyboardist Hector informed me, unfortunately, that he had to leave the group because Bo Diddly hired him and was leaving town the next week. This would not have been so devastating, except the P.A. system we were using was his and I did not own one. We discussed the situation at rehearsal one day, and he repeatedly told me how much he regretted leaving, as we had become a very tight group over the past months. Then he totally shocked me by saying, to show just how much he hated leaving us, he would be willing to sell me his sound system for a mere fifty dollars! I couldn't believe it, what a gift! I thanked him profusely, asked for an advance in my pay and paid him the fifty bucks.

One major hurdle cleared. The only thing remaining was finding a suitable replacement for Hector immediately. The other guys started recommending people they knew and I began scheduling auditions. It had to be someone who owned their own keyboard because there was not one in the restaurant. After a couple

Bob White and The White House with David Benoit at the keyboard in 1972.

of auditions, I still had not found someone to fill Hectors' shoes. Seemingly from out of nowhere, this young, skinny kid with long, stringy hair and wearing a multi-colored headband, walks in the club. No one knew who he was or where he came from. He walked up to me, smiled broadly and said, "Hi Bob, I'm David Benoit, I play keyboards and have my own Fender-Rhodes. I heard you are looking for a keyboardist and I would like to audition for you!" I looked him up and down, wondering how old he was but said, "Well, okay!" He said great, left to get his keyboard, returned and set it up. The other musicians were all there and we ran through our repertoire for the next hour or so. I was totally blown away! This kids' playing was beyond anything I could have imagined. He knew everything we were doing and could play in any key.

Afterwards, I ask him how old he was. He told me he was eighteen and had just finished high school. I knew I wanted to hire him without a doubt and told him so, but there was possibly one drawback, his age. I said I would have to check with the manager first to see if his age was going to be a problem. I approached the manager and told him my dilemma. He agreed to let me hire him, providing

David and I reunited in 2011.

that, when we were not on the bandstand playing, he would have to leave the club until we returned to play. I relayed this to David, he smiled in agreement and thanked me. David stayed with me and The White House until the conclusion of the job. On several Sundays after leaving The Polynesian, I went to his home in Manhattan Beach and jammed with him and his father, who played guitar. I stayed in touch with him for awhile, using him on other jobs when I could.

Since those humble beginnings, David's talent has carried him to the heights of musical recognition worldwide; a superstar, touring and recording with some of the best jazz musicians of our day, the recipient of numerous prestigious musical awards. His musical horizons have broadened to include arranging musical scores and conducting symphony orchestras as well as performing D.J. duties on classical and jazz music radio stations. With the many accolades David has received, he remains the down-to-earth young man I met in the early seventies, who took the time to acknowledge me and our musical relationship in the midst of one of his concerts I attended. No words can describe how proud I am of his accomplishments and how fortunate I am to have had the opportunity to work with such genius at the beginning of his ascent to heights still unknown.

Music was sustaining me in a meager way, but it was not sufficient to cover all my financial needs. Besides, it was not regular. There were periods where I had no work whatsoever. I was treading water and beginning to sink. As a result, I was applying for every regular job I thought I might be able to get; janitor, parking lot attendant, storekeeper or whatever. Some I knew I didn't qualify for such as police officer and fireman, but was just attracted by the salary. I took a job washing cars for a few weeks. Hell, it kept me from being evicted from the Bird Cage and helped appease those creditors temporarily.

I had received several notices informing me of a registered letter I had at the post office which I refused to go get, fearing some creditor was trying to sue me or I was going to jail for God knows what. One bright, sunny Friday I was feeling depressed and thought, what the hell, I'm going to the post office and get this damned letter and let whoever is after me, get me! I went and got the letter, walked outside, held the envelope up in the bright sunlight. Right away, I saw inside the envelope and written across the top, in big, bold black letters, were the words, LOS ANGELES POLICE DEPARTMENT. That scared the hell out of me. I just knew I was in big trouble for something and this was a warrant for my arrest.

Nervously, I drove home, opened the envelope and read the letter.

LAPD Wilshire Division.

It was congratulating me on being accepted for employment in the LOS ANGELES POLICE DEPARTMENT and if I chose to accept the job, report to the personnel department Monday morning at eight a.m. I was in complete disbelief, knowing a mistake had been made. I called the number listed in the letter immediately and asked if they were sure a mistake had not been made and if I had

Tom Bradley, Mayor of Los Angeles, during a fundraiser for underprivileged children.

truly passed all the tests. I was told a definite "Yes," and if I did not report on Monday, they would assume I had refused the position.

I reported, completed the academy and spent twenty-one years on the job, retiring just as the O.J. Simpson debacle was unfolding. Becoming a part of the police department was surely not a direction I planned to go, or gave the remotest thought to going, even though many of my boy scout and high school friends had became police officers and tried to convince me to do likewise over the years. It was not my cup of tea, but it was a regular job, with great benefits and pulled me out of the big hole that was consuming me, making my twilight years quite comfortable. I am very blessed.

I developed an interest in acting and enrolled in drama classes in a neighborhood drama workshop and El Camino Junior College, accepting roles in small theater productions. As a result, I became qualified to join the Screen Actors Guild. This opened the door for me to land a few small parts in movies, television shows and commercials.

I have received recognition as an award-winning artist with many of my drawings and paintings hanging in the homes of affluent people in California and other states throughout the U.S.

I am proud of my professional achievements, but more proud of my personal ones. My four children, one boy and three girls, are the joy of my life. They are all talented and have a great appreciation for the arts. My oldest daughter is a professional singer who sang in clubs locally, toured Japan, and was a guest performer on the Dinah Shore Television Show. She is now married with two children and still performs in church and for older residents in rest homes; my son toured with a European Theater Group throughout Europe in a production of Hair and West Side Story. He is still performing and pursuing his career in New York; and my second daughter is equally talented in the art field. She is a Computer Graphic Designer with Homeland Security, in charge of producing graphic displays for training purposes within the agency. My youngest daughter from a different relationship just completed college with a Liberal and Media Arts degree, and is working toward a career in the literary field. I expect great things from her in the future.

Let me add that life in my middle to late forties was very difficult and turbulent for me. I had been living the life of an entertainer, a Lounge Lizard and Star of the Bar, while going through mid-life crisis, although I didn't know what mid-life crisis was and had never heard of it. A few years earlier, I met and married my present wife and made her life a living hell. I talked constantly about quitting my job with the police department, stopping wearing socks and underwear and becoming a Hippie living on the beach. Suicide was something I thought of daily and slept with my gun under my pillow. My supervisor sent me home from work several times, strongly suggesting I get some therapy. I would break out crying uncontrollably for no reason whatsoever. I did start therapy sessions for six weeks at Kaiser and so did my wife, as well as with L.A.P.D.

My most effective therapy came from the department. It's affectionately called The Funny Farm where officers go for emotional problems after experiencing some traumatic situations on the job such as a shooting or something equally as upsetting.

Let me state very emphatically at this time in my memoir, how much I love and appreciate my wife for standing by me through all those hellish years she endured. I can never find the words to express my regret for treating her so unkindly. She has forgiven me completely. For this I will be forever grateful.

We have been happily married for thirty-three years. She has two sons from a previous marriage, and over the years we have successfully blended Hers and Mine to make for a happy family with the addition of six grandchildren. This phase of my life ends with the oldest story book ending in existence, "And They All Lived Happily Ever After!"

Although my artistic achievements are not acclaimed worldwide, I am content in knowing that an impoverished black boy who grew up deprived, overcame the obstacles of prejudice and poverty, discrimination and degradation, has received the satisfaction of knowing he achieved a small degree of success against overwhelming odds; satisfaction enough to be comfortable in also knowing his efforts were not all in vain, and that...

"He passed through this life, leaving something more than a footprint." For all this, I thank God, and for allowing me to grow up in a great country... The United States of America.

CENTER CLUB

May 23, 1998
Our Special Evening
with Bob White

Presenting celebrated Coach John Wooden of UCLA basketball with a copy of my pencil drawing of Mother Teresa in 2008.

Rap star and actor Ice Cube, during a break in filming of an independent film.

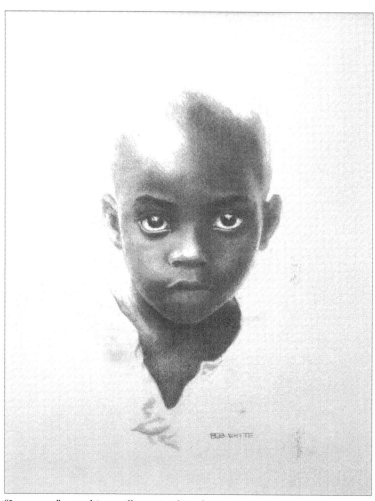

"Innocence" - graphite on illustration board.

"The Pause that Refreshes" - graphite on illustration board.

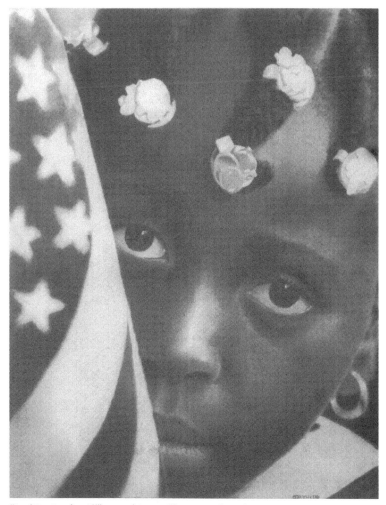

"And Justice for All" - graphite on illustration board.

"Mother Teresa" - graphite on illustration board.

"Ray Charles" - graphite on illustration board.

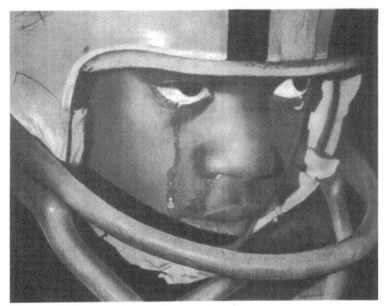

"Agony of Defeat" - graphite on illustration board.

"My Mother" - oil on canvas.

"Seascape" - oil on canvas.

Made in the USA
Charleston, SC
22 June 2011